Bathrooms

For all its importance in the modern home, the bathroom has been the last place to capture the imagination of creative designers. In this temple of hygiene, form has always been securely bound to sterile function, with plenty of gleaming fixtures, lots of scrubbable surfaces and yards of efficient pipe. But rarely in the past has the bath also been regarded as a splendid place to indulge the soul while cleansing the body.

No more. Today's marketplace of bathroom fixtures and furnishings brings extraordinary choices that range from rococo to streamlined, from sensuous to austere, from small scale to grand — double-wide bathtubs and minimal square tubs, corner washbasins and sculptured freestanding pedestal basins; golden faucets and crystal spouts. While pristine white and all its permutations from creamy ivory to pearly gray remain the best-selling colors, a rainbow of alternatives — including cherry red — awaits the adventurous.

Marble and tile have always been admirable materials for rooms full of steam and water; today they are joined by an expanding array of synthetics that look and feel luxurious but carry modest price tags. Mirrors, too, have multiplied and now cover walls, ceilings, even cabinets to create a sense of spaciousness. Some are glass — often safety glazed to resist shattering — while others are plastic or polished metals.

In the 10-page photographic prologue that follows, you will find a sampling of bathroom designs that make exciting use of these elements, underscoring them in some cases with the simple repetition of a basic motif or a sophisticated handling of natural and artificial lights. In the text and pictures that begin on page 16, you will learn how to assess your own goals for the bath and how to set about achieving them.

Curves — in the vaulted ceiling, in the arched window and doorway, in the countertop and, most important, in the unframed mirror over the basin — form a series of interacting arcs that draw together the disparate parts of this irregularly shaped bathroom. An angled window bench, itself backed by mirror, contributes comfort as well as extra storage space. And the pearly colors everywhere create an aura of cool composure.

cavernous old-style bathroom is turned
o a series of pleasantly intimate modern
mpartments, one for showering, one
dressing, and so on. The division is han-
d by crisp white canvas "sails" lashed
gleaming black floor-to-ceiling metal
mes. Glossy paints, shiny brass, mir-
ed glass, sparkling porcelain, and a deft
xture of indirect and task lighting com-
te the transformation.

A desire to preserve the spectacular view
outside a large window led to the custom design of this sleek vanity. The oak-veneer
cabinets are set low — level with the window
sill — and polyurethaned to shed water;
the stainless-steel washbasin rises to conventional height. At night, a window shade
recessed in a well at the back of the counter
is drawn up to provide privacy; the walls
and ceiling are mirrored to make the interi-
or space seem more expansive.

The unifying theme of this hospitable-looking bath is a tiny floral print, appearing as wallpaper on walls and ceiling, as fabric on the chair and the skirt that makes a vanity of the washbasin. The vanity top is water-resistant teak, into which are set an antique-style basin and hardware. The floral's main colors — ivory, brown and brick red — are repeated in picture frames, furniture, rugs and a Louis XV wall mirror.

Because this bathroom is tucked under the eaves, the only practical place for the tub is in the center; setting the tub on a dais gives bathing here a certain ceremonial air. Around it, Victorian furnishings create the ambiance of a cheery sitting room. A slender, painted towel rack matches the chair and dressing table *(at right)*, an antique chestnut cupboard *(back wall)* holds linens, and a sturdy walnut washstand next to the tub is topped with crockery holding soaps, brushes, fragrant herbs and the like. Rugged and moisture-safe jute matting carpets the floor.

Wrap-around mirrors — beveled panels on storage cabinets and drawers, plain panels on walls — brighten t recess enclosing two washbasins. Lighting floods from behind a concealed overhead soffit. Counter and basins are molded synthetic marble, outfitted with sleek gooseneck spigots and wide-flaring blade handles.

Hexagonal wall tiles and marble floors combine with mirror-finished stainless-steel partitions to give this room the look of a Roman bath. Partitions serve primarily to separate the bathing area from the toilet and shower units, but their arcs also emphasize the curves of the tub, of the oval stool, and of the circles of light that spill down the walls from the dimmer-controlled ceiling fixtures.

An undersized bathroom appears expansive through the skillful use of mirrors, glittering brass and chrome, creamy-colored marble and tile, and an amplitude of well-placed lighting. The washbasin and the looking glass above it are set cater-cornered, and single strips of warm-light incandescent tubes run along the inner folds of the mirror triptych, their light multiplying many times over.

The use of horizontal elements that lead the eye toward the window and beyond ma— dramatic virtue of this room's narrow shape: The cabinets create a continuous band along one wall, and the lengthwise mirror is topped with a lighting strip echoe— by a shelf strip below. Rectangular tiles on the floor and counter repeat the rectiline— theme. For nighttime brilliance, silver foil wraps walls and ceilings to make the bath fairly shine with reflected light.

Bathrooms

by the Editors of Time-Life Books

TIME-LIFE BOOKS □ ALEXANDRIA, VIRGINIA

YOUR HOME

THE CONSULTANTS

Library of Congress Cataloguing in
Publication Data
Main entry under title:
Bathrooms.

(Your home)
Includes index.
1. Bathrooms — Remodeling — Amateurs'
manuals. I. Time-Life Books. II. Series: Your
home (Alexandria, Va.)
TH6485.B374 1985   643'.52   85-16802
ISBN 0-8094-5533-1
ISBN 0-8094-5534-X

CONTENTS

The basics of bathroom planning

Although bathrooms are among the most private places in a home, they are nonetheless highly visible. Guests who are in your home for more than a few hours are likely to visit a bathroom. Chances are that a bathroom is your first stop after getting up in the morning and your last before going to bed at night. And if you enjoy lingering in a hot bath, you probably spend a lot of your bathroom time idly inspecting the surroundings.

Naturally, you want any room so frequently on display to be attractive as well as useful, to satisfy your personal taste while fulfilling its practical role. This book can help you achieve that goal for your bathroom. It will tell you how to transform a bathroom's appearance with mirrors, tiles, or paint that mimics marble. You will discover ways to add shelves and other forms of storage, to improve lighting, to replace old, worn fittings with new, stylish ones.

If you wish to completely remodel your bathroom, or create a new one where none was before, the first step is careful planning. More and stronger strictures affect the planning of a bathroom than of any other room. Two of the prime elements that must be taken into account are space (almost always very limited) and plumbing (which must be configured in accordance with physical laws as well as

with those of the community). These factors are discussed on page 19. The other chief consideration is the fixtures.

Bathroom fixtures work hard. A tub handles about 3 gallons of water per bath — keeping the water hot, providing safe footing and comfortable seating for the bathe emptying efficiently so almost all the dirt goes down th drain instead of sticking to the tub surface. A toilet servir a family of four is operated about 6,000 times a year, flush ing down 36,500 gallons of water along with the wastes.

Fixtures should also be pleasant to look at, since the usually provide a bathroom's visual focus. The possibili ties for combining the ideals of efficiency and attractive ness are greater today than ever before: Numerous form colors and materials are available. No one material is pe fect for all fixtures (although vitreous china — a mixture clays and glass resistant to strong acids, smooth-surface and easy to clean — has never been surpassed for toilets i its century of use). The advantages and drawbacks of di ferent substances used in fixtures and countertops are de scribed in the chart below. That chart, and the drawings o the next two pages showing the basic forms in which fix tures are available, will tell you what to look for when yo begin surveying plumbing showrooms and catalogues.

A Choice of Materials

Materials	Tubs	Showers	Toilets and Bidets	Basins	Advantages	Disadvantages
Cast iron clad in 1/16″ porcelain enamel	●			●	Very strong; long-lasting. Glossy, chip-resistant finish. Quiet. Keeps water hot. Many colors.	Very heavy: 350 to 500 lbs. for average tub. Expensive to ship and handle.
Enameled steel	●			●	Strong; long-lasting. Medium weight: 120 lbs. for average tub. Moderate cost. Glossy finish. Many colors.	Chips easily. Noisy. Does not keep water hot.
Fiberglass-reinforced plastics	●	●		●	Moderately strong. Lightweight: 60 to 70 lbs. for average tub. Moderate cost. Moderate noise. Seamless bath or shower surround, easy to install and clean. Warm to the touch. Half a dozen colors.	Finish dulls with use. Subject to stress cracking. Easily scratched and charred. Does not keep water hot. Requires nonabrasive cleanser.
Vitreous china			●	●	Strong; long-lasting. Moderate cost. Glossy acid-resistant finish. Many colors.	Subject to chipping and stress cracking.
Acrylic-based simulated marble (Corian®)				●	Strong; long-lasting. Translucent. Burns and scars can be easily removed with abrasives.	Very heavy. Few colors.
Polyester-based simulated marble				●	Moderately strong; long-lasting. Moderate cost. Many colors.	Subject to staining, scratching, charring, crazing. Requires nonabrasive cleanser.
Ceramic tile	●	●			Strong; long-lasting. Used for custom shapes. Glossy or mat chip-resistant finish. Quiet. Keeps water hot. Many colors and patterns.	Heavy. Requires professional installation. Grout subject to mildew. Cracks under impact.

Tub and Shower Styles

Bathtubs can be purchased in many different shapes and sizes. The old-fashioned 6-foot-long claw-footed tub has had a renaissance. A standard 5-foot-long rectangular tub may come without finished outer sides so it can be sunk into a floor or platform, or with one, two or three finished outer sides, depending on how many walls the tub will abut. A 4-foot-by-4-foot tub called a receptor or the slightly smaller 43-inch-long corner unit is suitable for a child or a seated adult and can be fitted with a shower stall. Oversize whirlpool tubs, which hold a lot of water, may require reinforcing the floor and putting in a larger water heater and bigger pipes.

Plastic showers and shower-tub combinations come in one-piece modules or in easy-to-install sections. Standard shower stalls are 30- or 36-inch squares or 36-by-48-inch rectangles. Among the nonstandard options are circular and corner units.

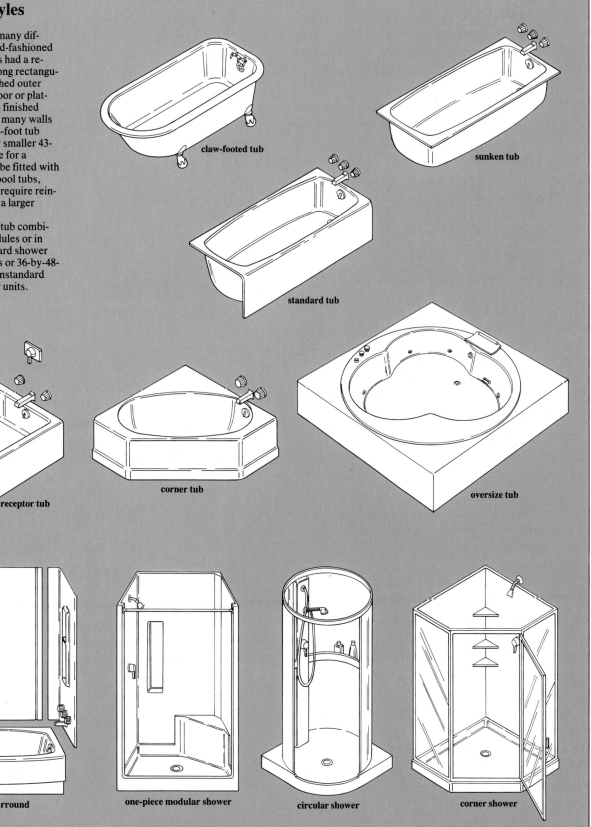

claw-footed tub

sunken tub

standard tub

receptor tub

corner tub

oversize tub

multi-piece tub surround

one-piece modular shower

circular shower

corner shower

Toilet and Bidet Styles

The two-piece floor-mounted toilet has long been the standard. The one-piece floor-mounted toilet combines the advantages of a nonoverflow feature, a quiet flushing action, and a compactness that frees wall space for shelves or cabinets. A wall-hung toilet can be secured at a nonstandard height and makes it easy to clean the floor below. A corner toilet with a triangular flush tank gives ample elbow space even in a small room and saves on water use.

Bidets are available in floor-mounted or wall-hung versions to match the toilets they accompany.

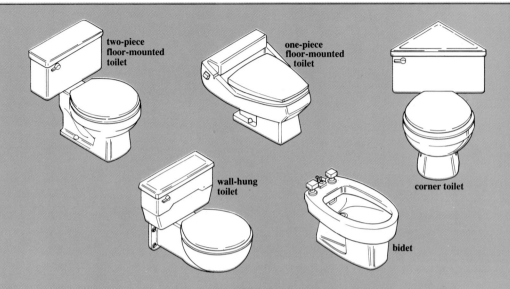

two-piece floor-mounted toilet

one-piece floor-mounted toilet

corner toilet

wall-hung toilet

bidet

Washbasin Styles

Bathroom washbasins are mounted on pedestals, on walls or in countertops. A pedestal hides the drainpipe without crowding the room, while a wall-hung basin leaves even more free space. (The corner basin at far right is a wall-hung unit.)

The best countertop bowls are integrated into the counter without a seam or are self-rimmed models that drop into the counter. The installation of metal-rimmed and recessed countertop basins creates seams and crevices that are difficult to keep clean. Bowls come in many designs: round, oval, D-shaped, rectangular, triangular and hexagonal.

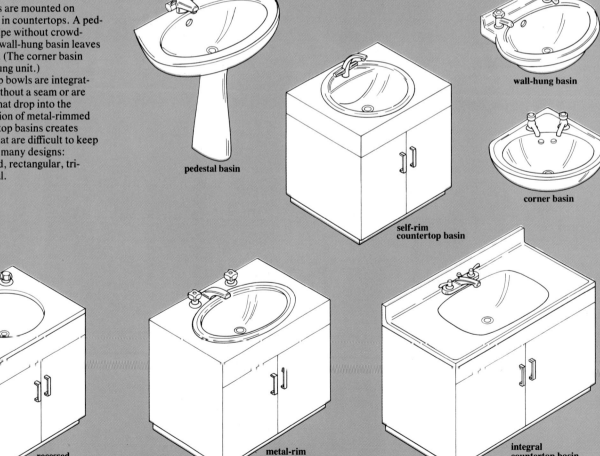

pedestal basin

wall-hung basin

self-rim countertop basin

corner basin

recessed countertop basin

metal-rim countertop basin

integral countertop basin

itting It All Together

efore planning a new bathroom, you ed a basic understanding of a typical umbing system *(right),* as well as a fa-iliarity with fixture dimensions and with ws that affect where you are allowed to it them *(below, left and right).*

When fixtures are side by side and umbing is concentrated along a wall, e room is said to have one "wet wall." hanges that create a second or third wet all require running pipes under the floor d add work and expense.

A basin is the easiest — and least cost-— fixture to move. A tub or shower sts more, and most expensive of all is e toilet, because of its large waste pipe.

Standard heights for fixtures and ac-ssories *(below, left)* can be adjusted to it those who use the bathroom most, it avoid radical departures. Fixtures wered for a four-year-old, for example, ill outlast their usefulness at that level; a ooden stand for the child is preferable.

Each fixture needs free space around it allow room for use and cleaning. Mini-um clearances are mandated by local uilding codes; be sure to check your ea's code if you are adding or moving xtures or building a new bathroom.

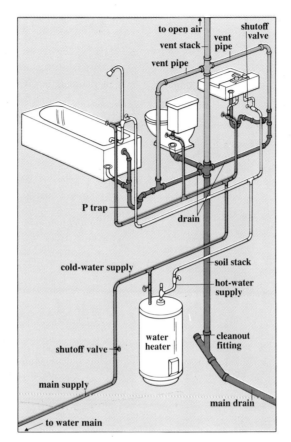

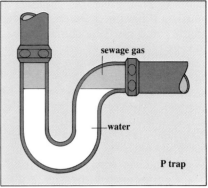

Fundamental plumbing. Four networks of pipes keep a bathroom operating. Two of them, cold *(green)* and hot *(white)* supply pipes, feed water to the fixtures under pressure. Shutoff valves can stop the flow when necessary. Gravity carries waste water away through another network *(dark gray),* made up of slanting drainpipes and the vertical soil stack into which they empty. Under basin and tub and inside the toilet, bends in the drains, known as P traps *(above),* remain full of water to prevent sewage gases in the drains from escaping into the room. Instead, the gases leave the house through the fourth network *(light gray),* the vent pipes and vent stack. The vent system also keeps drains at atmospheric pressure, to prevent partial vacuums that could retard drainage.

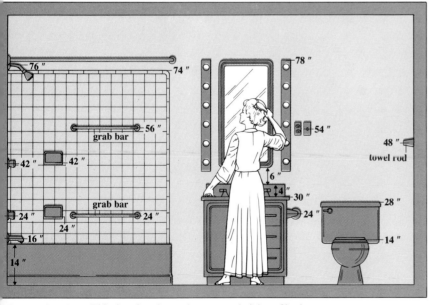

athroom elevations. This drawing shows the average heights of bath-om fixtures and the usual distances above the floor for common fittings d accessories. These measurements are based on architectural stan-rds intended to accommodate people from about 5 feet tall to 6 feet 3 ches. If not instructed otherwise, a contractor creating a bathroom ill apply these standards. But measurements can be adjusted to suit the athroom's principal users. The height of basin and vanity top can be ised, for instance, by installing the vanity on a wood frame, or lowered / sawing off part of the vanity's base. A wall-mounted toilet could be aced higher or lower than the floor-mounted model shown here.

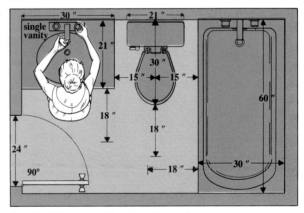

Standard clearances. The shaded areas in this picture represent the minimum clearances around fixtures mandated by local building codes; the dimensions of the fixtures themselves describe average sizes. Codes usually require at least 18 inches in front of each fixture and 15 inches to each side of a toilet's center line. A door must be no less than 24 inches wide and must open through an arc of at least 90°. These are minimum requirements. More liberal space allowances should be provided if possible.

A Portfolio of Designs

Room size is the most important factor in bathroom planning, since it limits the number and size of fixtures, how much storage you can have, and the scope for extra features. If you are creating a new bathroom or wish to move or add fixtures, start by determining the space available. Measure the room and its fixtures, and make scale drawings of the floor plan and of each wall on graph paper. Note which way the door swings; include windows, lights and electrical outlets, ventilation and heating units; and show adjacent closets and hallways. (You might decide to expand into one of those areas; a larger bathroom may be worth the sacrifice of a little-used hall closet.)

Consult fixture catalogues and the guide to fixture types on pages 16-18. Cut pieces of paper to scale to represent the fixtures you think you want, and try placing them in different arrangements on your scale drawings. As you experiment, keep in mind clearance requirements and what each scheme would entail in plumbing work (page 19).

Consider accessories and other features at the same time that you are plotting fixture schemes. Think about mirrors, cabinets, and floor and wall treatments in relation to the fixtures. What about a skylight? A window loaded with greenery? What kind of lighting would suit your scheme?

You will find some tips about making the best use of space in the bathroom plans presented here and on the following pages. They show different ways to treat rooms ranging from the very small (4½ feet by 5½ feet) to the — for bathrooms — very grand (13 feet by 14 feet). They vary in the style and expense of fixtures involved, and in the special purposes the bathrooms serve: One doubles as an exercise room, another as a laundry. (Note that all these rooms have ceiling lights and exhaust fans that are not shown in the bird's-eye-view drawings.)

Another excellent source for ideas and advice is a professional bathroom planner. A planner with years of technical training and experience can cut through problems quickly. Even an hour or two of a professional's time is well worth the fee if you come away with just the space-saving idea you need or with a custom-tailored solution to a more general bathroom planning problem.

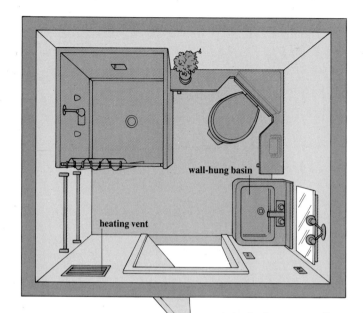

A simple shower room. Even a 4½-by-5½-foot cubicle is large enough for a shower room when fitted with space-saving fixtures. The molded plastic shower is the minimum, 30-inch-square size permitted by code. The corner toilet allows greater clearances than a normal toilet and makes room for a generous shelf stretching around the corner (the shelf lifts off supporting brackets to provide access to the toilet tank). A wall-hung basin, a recessed medicine chest and a door that opens outward — permitted only if it opens into a room, not a hallway — help create the impression of uncrowded space.

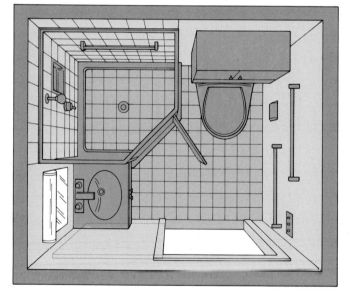

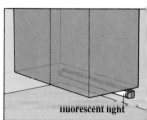

A touch of luxury. In a room the same size as the one at top, the expenditure of more money produces quite a different effect. Ceramic tiles smarten up the floor and the shower walls. A glass shower enclosure keeps the area within visually part of the room. Storage is plentiful both in a cabinet high above the toilet and in a vanity that conceals the basin plumbing. The vanity also serves as a special visual feature: Hung on the wall, it appears to float on the glow from an unseen fluorescent light beneath it (detail, above). A pocket door demands no space from the room; it slides into the wall to open.

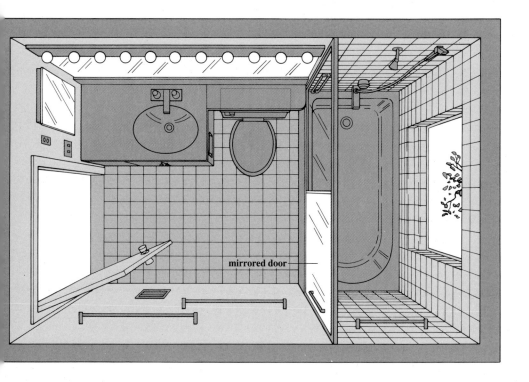

A bathroom that works well. Function is the primary consideration in the 5-by-8-foot bathroom at left. Durability and easy maintenance characterize not only the ceramic-tile floor and bath-enclosure walls but also the enameled cast-iron tub, which includes a hand shower that facilitates cleaning. An acrylic-based simulated-marble countertop with integral basin and backsplash presents a smooth, continuous surface that is easy to clean, while the big vanity below provides ample storage. Theatrical lights give even illumination for make-up. A large mirror on the vanity wall and a mirrored sliding-door panel of the tub enclosure make the room appear more spacious.

mirrored door

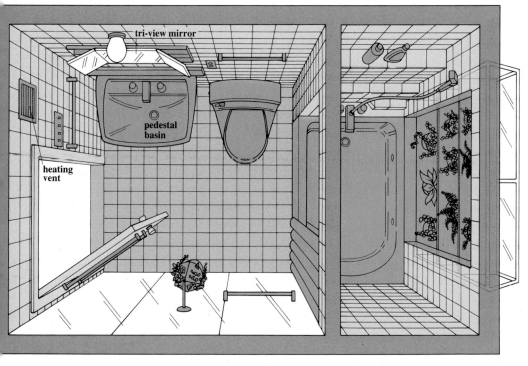

An indoor garden. Here, shelves festooned with plants in a sun-catching shallow bay window make a greenhouse of a tub compartment. Although this bathroom, like the one pictured above it, is only 5 feet by 8 feet — little larger than average — the garden window and other special features qualify it as exceptionally luxurious. The tub is 24 inches deep, with a whirlpool system; it is sunk in a tiled deck with stair-step shelves for bath articles. Outside the tub area, the floor and three of the walls are also tiled, while the fourth wall is completely covered by sections of mirror that virtually double the apparent size of the room.

tri-view mirror

pedestal basin

heating vent

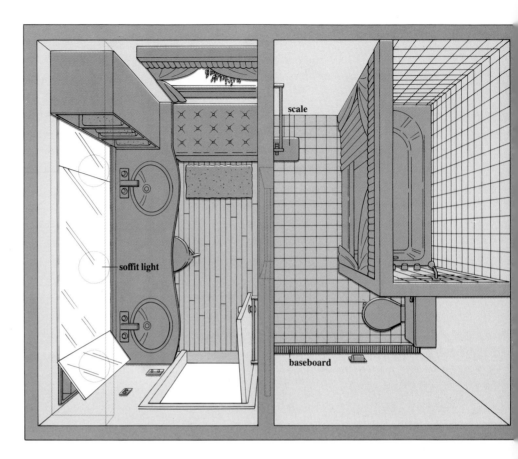

Two rooms in one. The generous size of an 8-by-10-foot room allows for dividing the space, creating a comfortably appointed dressing compartment on one side of a partition while keeping toilet and tub out of sight on the other side. In the dressing area, warmth and softness are expressed in the curves of the laminate counter, the curtains framing a pretty view, a cushioned window seat and a scatter rug on a wood-strip floor. A wall of mirrors behind the twin basins — including two mirrored doors of recessed medicine cabinets — gives the compartment more visual space, and a soffit conceals lighting over the counter.

Beyond a pocket door, the wood floor yields to more functional tile, but a valanced shower curtain carries the charm of the dressing room into this section, too. When not in use, the scale folds up into the wall.

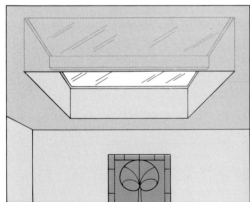

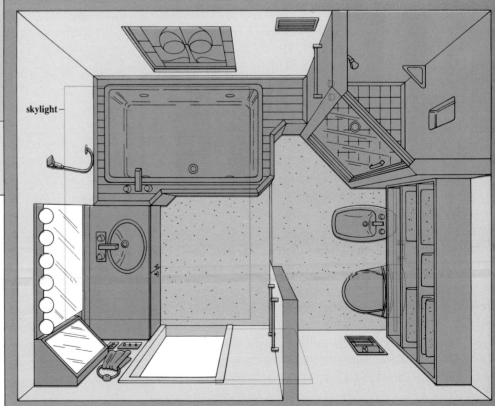

A treat for the eyes. Natural light, pouring through an outsize skylight *(detail, above)* and a stained-glass window, illuminates the tub's redwood deck and apron, presenting an eye-pleasing scene to anyone passing the open door of this bathroom. A carpeted floor is equally pleasing to bare feet. A glass-doored shower stall supplements the big whirlpool tub, with plenty of space left over for a bidet alongside the low, streamlined toilet. When night darkens the skylight, theatrical lights bring even brightness to the vanity corner, and lights recessed in the ceiling *(not shown)* shine down on tub, shower, toilet and bidet.

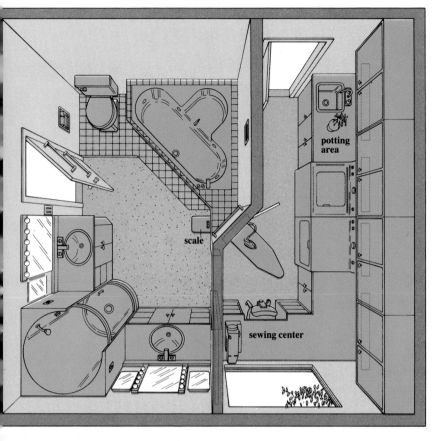

potting area

scale

sewing center

Bath plus laundry. Because of the economies of concentrating plumbing, another excellent candidate for sharing bathroom space is the laundry, particularly when the functions can be separated, as in this 13-by-14-foot room. Here, the sunny washing and ironing section also provides a potting area near the sink, a sewing center facing the window, and cabinets galore. A light in the recessed ironing-board cabinet shines on the extended board, which folds away when not in use.

The master bath remains ample and warm, with his and her vanities, a vast whirlpool sunk in a ceramic-tile deck, and a circular shower. Extra touches are a fold-away bathroom scale near the tub and a recessed magazine rack by the toilet. The floor in the bath compartment is carpeted while that in the laundry room is a no-wax sheet vinyl.

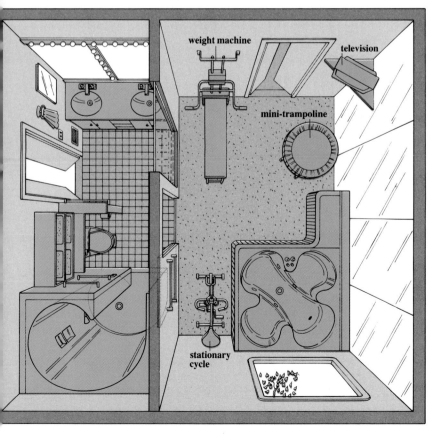

weight machine

television

mini-trampoline

stationary cycle

Bath plus gym. Here, a bedroom has been used to create an extra-large bathroom: 13 feet by 14 feet. (The rooms on this page are drawn on a smaller scale than those opposite.) Thus, part of the space can be devoted to another use — in this case, exercising on a mini-trampoline, a weight machine and a stationary cycle. Two entrances and a partition with a pocket door allow the two areas to be used at the same time. A whirlpool bath provides both relaxation after a workout and a good view of the television, which is wall-mounted and remote-controlled for safety. On the other side of the partition, the spiral shape of the shower stall makes a shower door or curtain unnecessary. The floor is carpeted in the exercise area and tiled in the shower and lavatory compartment.

Replacing fittings and fixtures

Unlike most rooms, a bathroom seems furnished with immovable objects. In fact, washbasins, while difficult to relocate, are easily replaced with modern versions in the same styles, with ready-made vanity cabinets and countertops *(pages 38-41)*, or with basins mounted in such furniture as a chest of drawers *(pages 42-48)* or a side table *(pages 50-51)*.

Furthermore, any basin, old or new, can be made more attractive by upgrading its faucet — the handles and spout *(pages 27-31)*. Because all basin fittings, including drain flange, pop-up plug, trap, supply pipes and valves, are readily accessible, you can match them to the new faucet.

By contrast, the plumbing for bathtubs and showers is buried in the wall; replacing it requires major remodeling. The exposed bathtub and shower handles, tub spouts, shower heads, drain covers and plugs, however, are easily changed *(pages 34-37)*, and come in as many styles and materials — brass, chrome, porcelain, even gold — as do basin fittings.

The first step in any of these undertakings is selecting the fittings and fixtures. There are three basic types of washbasin faucets: wide-spread sets, such as the Victorian reproduction at right, center sets and single-hole sets *(page 26)*. You need one that fits the spacing of your washbasin's existing side holes, measured between the centers of the handles. For a wide-spread set, the side holes can be 6 to 20 inches apart, for a center set, 4 inches apart. For a single-hole mount, the base plate should be long enough to cover the side holes.

Installation methods vary, but all are largely a matter of positioning the faucet on the basin and connecting its pieces. Drain configurations also vary, but most include one or more slip-nut connections easily dismantled with a wrench. A one-piece adjustable swivel trap that permits drain connection to vary horizontally by as much as inches *(pages 32-33)* can replace an old two-piece swivel trap. In addition, the trap's drainpipe can be adjusted i size to bridge the distance between the wall connectio and the basin's drain opening.

Plumbing suppliers sell slip-joint extension tubes for ac justing the length of a drain tailpiece, and waste connector for adapting the drainpipe connection to accept a one piece adjustable swivel trap. To replace only a drain flang and pop-up plug, remove the trap first. If it is reusable, pu new washers under the slip nuts when reassembling it.

While the systems shown on the following pages are th most common, you may encounter others. You will fin help at a plumbing-supply store, where you also can rer plumbing tools, such as the basin wrench *(page 27)* de signed for work in tight quarters behind a washbasin.

At least several hours before you disconnect an old fat cet or drain fittings, spray all the threaded connection with penetrating lubricant. Before joining pipes, wra plumbing-sealant tape around the threads to lubricate an seal them, and also to protect them from corrosion.

After removing an old faucet and before installing a new one, clean the washbasin with a solution of equal parts c white vinegar and water to dissolve the crusty remains c water minerals. A poultice of cream of tartar and hydroge peroxide removes rust stains from vitreous china.

When the installation is completed, test for leaks b closing the drain, filling the basin with water, then openin the drain. Slightly tighten any leaking connections.

Caution: A plumbing permit is not usually needed whe replacing an existing fixture does not alter the system Check your local plumbing inspector if questions arise.

Wide-Spread Faucet

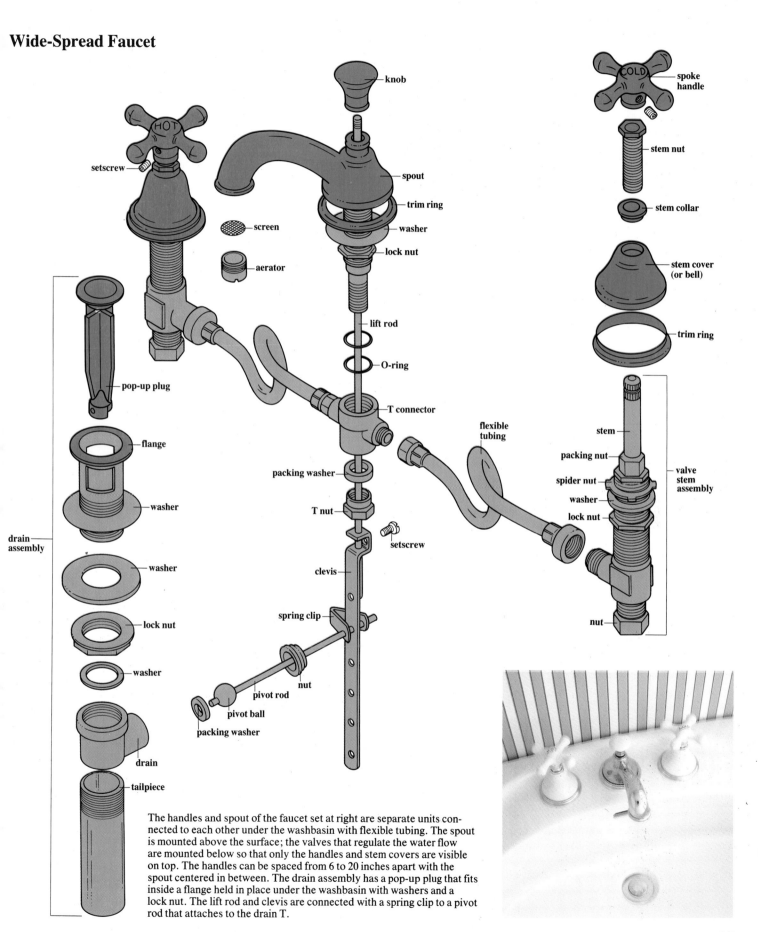

knob

spoke handle

COLD

HOT

setscrew

spout

trim ring

screen

washer

lock nut

aerator

stem nut

stem collar

stem cover (or bell)

trim ring

pop-up plug

lift rod

O-ring

T connector

flexible tubing

stem

packing nut

spider nut

washer

lock nut

valve stem assembly

flange

washer

packing washer

T nut

setscrew

clevis

washer

lock nut

washer

spring clip

nut

pivot rod

pivot ball

packing washer

drain assembly

nut

drain

tailpiece

The handles and spout of the faucet set at right are separate units connected to each other under the washbasin with flexible tubing. The spout is mounted above the surface; the valves that regulate the water flow are mounted below so that only the handles and stem covers are visible on top. The handles can be spaced from 6 to 20 inches apart with the spout centered in between. The drain assembly has a pop-up plug that fits inside a flange held in place under the washbasin with washers and a lock nut. The lift rod and clevis are connected with a spring clip to a pivot rod that attaches to the drain T.

A Center-Set Faucet

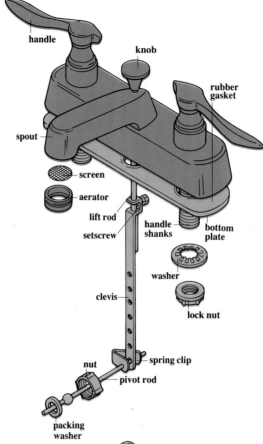

handle

knob

rubber gasket

spout

screen

aerator

lift rod

setscrew

handle shanks

bottom plate

washer

clevis

lock nut

nut

spring clip

pivot rod

packing washer

Two valves, handles and a spout constitute this faucet that is installed above the surface of the washbasin using three separate holes — a center hole for the pop-up lift rod and two side holes for the faucet shanks, which are spaced 4 inches apart. The faucet is connected to the water supply pipes beneath the washbasin. Its drain apparatus, not shown, is like that of a wide-spread set (page 25).

A Single-Hole Faucet

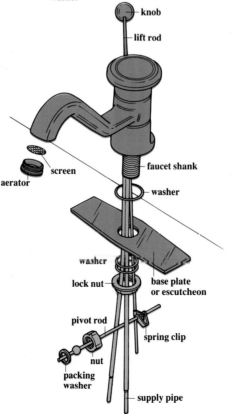

knob

lift rod

screen

aerator

faucet shank

washer

washer

lock nut

base plate or escutcheon

pivot rod

spring clip

nut

packing washer

supply pipe

Only one hole is needed for the pop-up lift rod and a pair of water supply pipes. The semiflexible supply pipes connect with the shutoff valves underneath the basin. This type of faucet can be used to replace a center-set faucet, providing the center hole in the basin is large enough; the base plate or escutcheon of the single-hole faucet covers the unused side holes. The drain assembly, not shown, resembles the one for the wide-spread set (page 25).

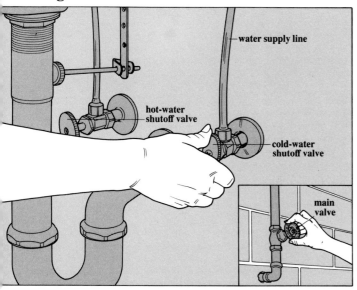

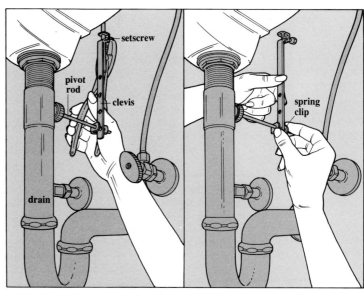

1 Turning off the water supply. Before disconnecting a faucet, turn off the hot-water and cold-water shutoff valves below the basin *(above)*. If the shutoffs' handles will not turn or if your bathroom does not have individual shutoffs for the fixture, you will have to turn off the main valve *(inset)*, typically located next to an indoor water meter or where the water supply enters the house. Then drain the entire system; open faucets at both the highest and lowest points in the house — the top floor and the basement — in order to prevent a vacuum from forming in the system and blocking the flow of water.

2 Freeing the pop-up plug mechanism. With pliers, loosen the setscrew securing the pop-up lift rod to the clevis, or adapter bar, located behind the drain underneath the basin *(above, left)*. From above the basin, pull the lift rod up and out of the clevis. With your fingers, pinch the spring clip holding the pivot rod in place on the clevis *(above, right)*, and pull the clevis and spring clip free.

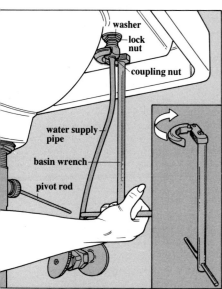

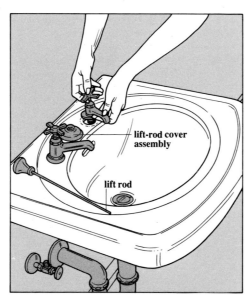

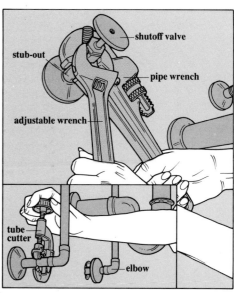

3 Disconnecting the water supply pipes. With a basin wrench *(inset)*, unscrew the coupling nut that attaches the top of one water supply pipe to a faucet shank. Slide the coupling nut down the supply pipe. Then unscrew the lock nut holding the pipe to the faucet shank, and remove the nut and its washer. Finally, unscrew the coupling nut at the bottom of the supply pipe to separate the line from the shutoff valve. Disconnect the other supply pipe similarly.

4 Removing cover assembly and faucet. With the basin wrench, unscrew the lock nut under the basin that anchors the lift-rod cover assembly. Then lift the faucet handles and cover assembly out of the basin.

5 Removing old shutoff valves. Look beneath the washbasin to see how the old fittings are connected. Unscrew old threaded shutoffs *(above)* or elbows with two wrenches: one to hold the stub-out, and one to turn the valve or elbow. Use a tube cutter to cut off soldered elbows, used with copper pipe, between the wall and the elbow *(inset)*. If other old fittings are unsightly or do not work properly, remove the pop-up, drains and trap *(pages 32-33)*.

Installing a Wide-Spread Faucet

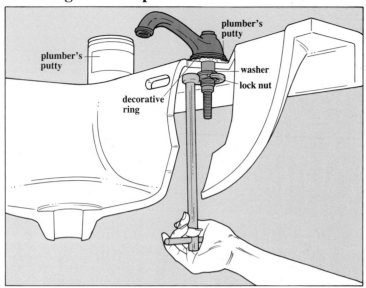

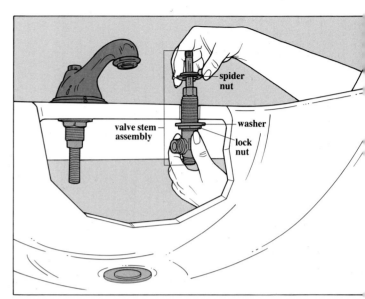

1 **Mounting the faucet spout.** Press a pencil-thick bead of plumber's putty around the edges of the underside of the spout of a wide-spread faucet. Insert the shank of the spout through the decorative ring and into the center hole of the washbasin. Position the spout at right angles to the back of the basin. Then use a basin wrench to secure the spout to the washbasin with a washer and lock nut. Scrape away any excess putty from around the spout with your finger.

2 **Installing valve-stem assemblies.** Place a washer and lock nut on the stem body of the cold-water valve. From underneath the washbasin, p the stem through the right-hand hole *(above)*. With your fingers, screw a spider nut on the top of the valve. Adjust the upper and lower nuts so that the stem body protrudes above the washbasin surface by the distance recommended by the manufacturer — here, 2 thread widt Install the hot-water valve in the same way.

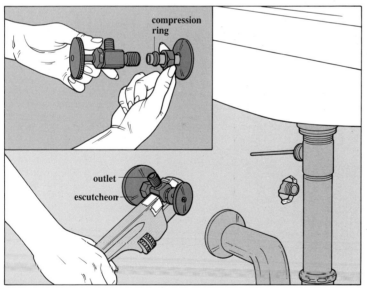

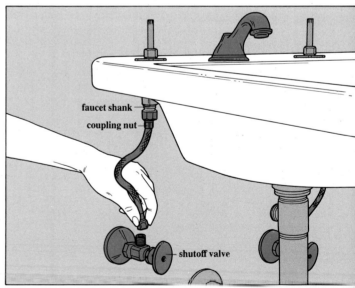

5 **Installing shutoff valves.** Slide an escutcheon of the appropriate size and finish against the wall over each stub-out. Wrap the threads of the stub-outs with a layer of plumbing-sealant tape. Using your hand, screw new shutoff valves onto the stub-outs. Then, with a crescent wrench or, as shown here, a pipe wrench, tighten the valves until the outlets face upward. On unthreaded copper stub-outs, use shutoff valves with compression connections *(inset)*.

6 **Attaching flexible supply pipes.** Wrap plumbing-sealant tape around the threads of both faucet shanks and both shutoff valves. Insert a wash into each of the larger coupling nuts. On each side of the washbasin, hand-tighten the larger coupling nut of a supply pipe to the faucet shank and the smaller coupling nut to the shutoff. Tighten each nut one half turn beyond hand-tight with an adjustable wrench. Do not overtighten.

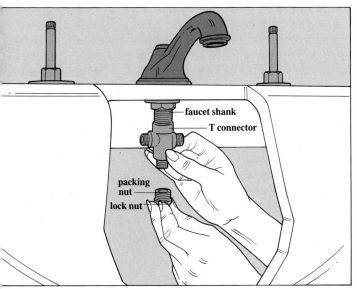

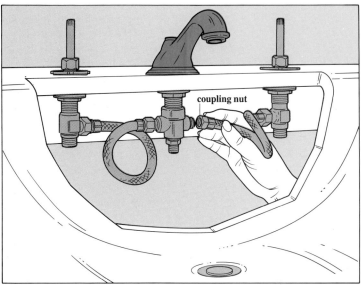

3 **Attaching the T connector.** Place an O-ring and washer on the upper side of the T connector for the faucet set. Slip the T connector onto the shank of the spout *(above)* and thread on the lock nut with a packing washer above it. Hand-tighten, then use a wrench to make the nut secure.

4 **Connecting spout and stem bodies.** Wrap a layer of plumbing-sealant tape around the threads on the T connector and each stem body. Hand-tighten the larger coupling nut of the flexible pipe to the valve-stem body and the smaller coupling nut to the T connector *(above)*. With an adjustable wrench, make a final turn on each nut.

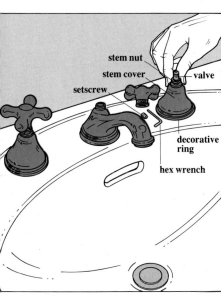

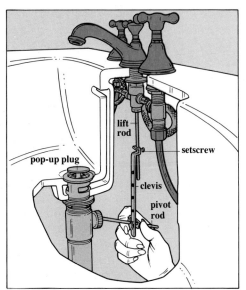

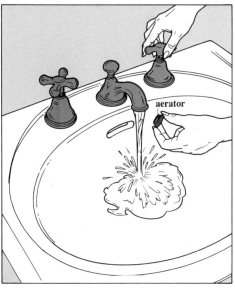

7 **Installing spoke handles.** Place a decorative ring and stem cover over each stem body. Secure each cover by hand with a stem nut. Temporarily slip the handles onto the stems and turn each one to the off position. Remove the handles, then reposition them on the stems so that the **H** and **C** markers are properly aligned with the back of the basin. Then tighten the setscrew in each handle with a hex wrench.

8 **Installing the lift rod.** Drop the lift rod through the hole in the spout. From underneath the basin, slip the lift rod through the holes in the top of the clevis. Insert the pivot rod into the clevis and pull both downward to raise the pop-up plug in the drain *(above)*. If necessary, move the pivot rod to a different hole in the clevis. Then lock the lift rod in place by fastening the setscrew at the top of the clevis.

9 **Flushing out the faucet.** Unscrew the aerator, an attachment in the underside of the spout that ensures an even flow of water and prevents splashing. Turn on the water at the shutoff valves. Turn the hot- and cold-water handles to full force to clear the faucet of sediment. While the water is running, check each connection under the washbasin. If you spot a leak, tighten the connection slightly with a wrench. Then turn off the water and replace the aerator.

Installing a Center-Set Faucet

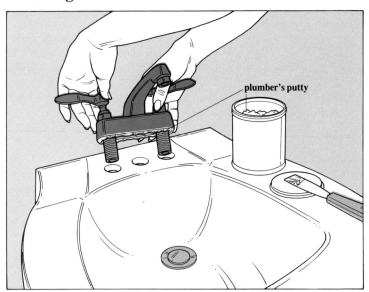

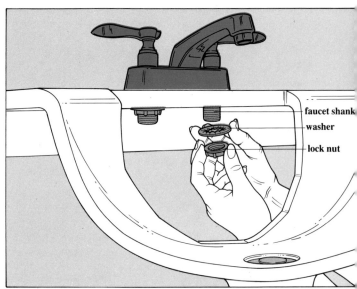

1 **Inserting the faucet.** Spread a layer of plumber's putty on the underside of the faucet body. Or, if the faucet manufacturer provides a watertight rubber gasket and bottom plate, slip them over the faucet shanks. Next, insert the shanks into the appropriate holes in the basin.

2 **Securing the faucet.** Slip a washer onto one of the faucet shanks. Thread on a lock nut and hand-tighten it against the underside of the washbasin. Attach a washer and lock nut to the other shank in the same manner. Then tighten both lock nuts with a basin wrench to secure the faucet firmly to the washbasin.

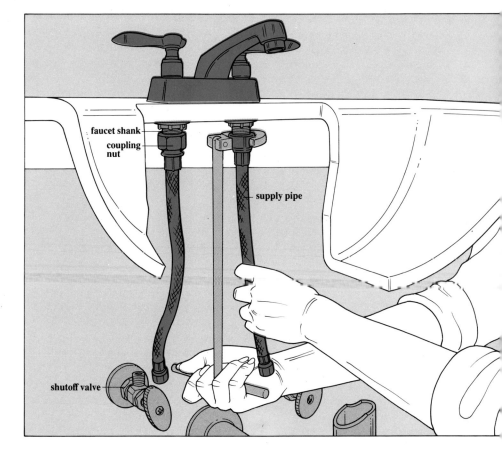

3 **Attaching flexible supply pipes.** Wrap plumbing-sealant tape around the threads of the faucet shanks and shutoff valves. Insert a washer into each of the large coupling nuts of the supply pipe and hand-tighten them to the faucet shanks. Then attach the smaller coupling nuts to the shutoff valves. Make a final half turn on each nut with a basin wrench. Turn on the water at the shutoffs. Remove the aerator from the spout, turn the water on at the faucet and flush it out. Meanwhile, check under the basin for leaks *(page 29, Step 9)*.

Installing a Single-Hole Faucet

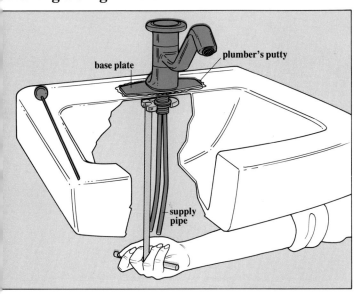

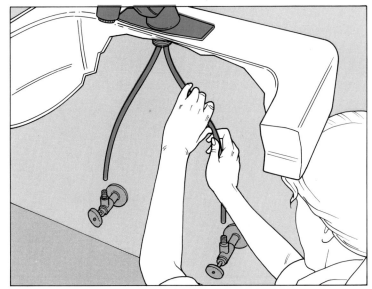

1 **Installing the faucet.** Spread plumber's putty on the underside of the base plate. Center the plate over the hole at the back of the basin, aligning it with the wall. Insert the faucet and supply pipes through the hole in the base plate without bending or separating the pipes. Press the base plate down. Under the basin, push a washer up over the pipes. Thread a lock nut onto the faucet shank and tighten it with a basin wrench *(above)*.

2 **Bending the supply pipes.** With your hands, separate the two water supply pipes hanging below the basin. Work gently; if you bend the pipe sharply, it will crimp and the faucet will become useless. Put your thumbs together *(above)* and shape one of the pipes at a time into a gentle curve that lines up with one of the shutoff valves.

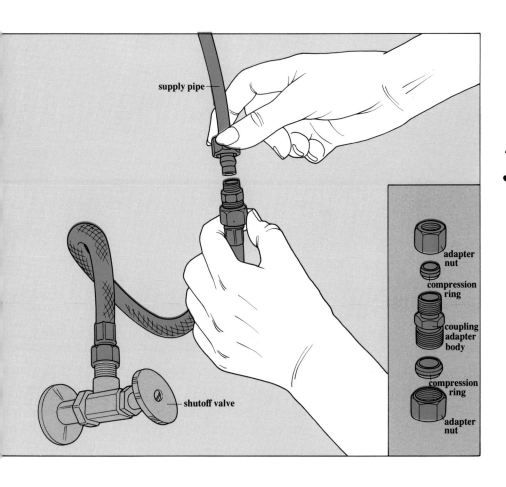

3 **Using transition fittings.** If the faucet's supply pipes do not reach the shutoff valves, use flexible pipes to connect them to the valves. Wrap the threads of a compression coupling adapter *(inset)* with plumbing-sealant tape. Slip a small adapter nut, followed by a compression ring, onto one faucet supply pipe. Screw the larger nut and ring followed by the coupling-adapter body onto one end of the flexible pipe. Connect the coupling adapter to the ring-and-nut assembly on the supply pipe. Connect the other end of the pipe to the shutoff valve with a coupling nut. Repeat this procedure to connect the other supply pipe. Open the valves, flush out the faucet and check for leaks *(page 29, Step 9)*.

31

Pop-up Drain Plugs

Each of the three types of plugs shown below performs the same job, although it fits differently in a drain. The plug at the left sits atop the pivot rod and can be lifted directly out of the drain. The center plug cannot be removed; it is permanently secured in the drain by a ring that engages the pivot rod. If you wish to replace this type of plug, you must remove the pivot rod from the drain T under the basin. To remove the plug at the right, you must free it by giving the body a quarter turn.

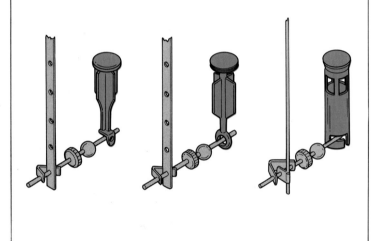

Putting in New Drains and Traps

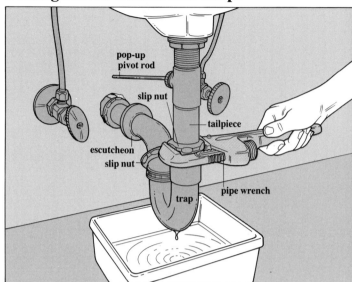

1 **Removing the trap.** Place a shallow container underneath the trap to catch the water contained in the trap. Pull the pipe escutcheon from the wall and unscrew the slip nut behind it at the wall connection. With a pipe wrench, unscrew the slip nuts on both ends of the trap *(above)*. Pull the trap down off the drain tailpiece and drainpipe. If it cannot be pulled down easily, unscrew the drain tailpiece from the drain and push it down inside the trap; then remove the trap. With pliers, unscrew the retaining nut on the back of the drain T and remove the pivot rod.

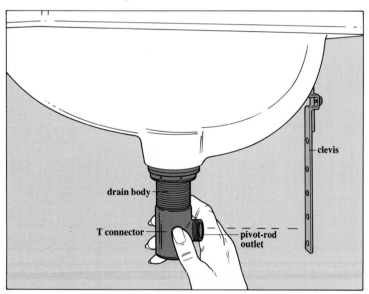

4 **Aligning the drain T.** Wrap plumbing-sealant tape around the threads on the lower part of the drain body. Screw the drain T onto the drain body so that the pivot-rod outlet on the T faces the clevis *(above)*. Insert the pivot rod into the drain T and the clevis. Tighten the nut on the drain T and adjust the spring clip on the clevis.

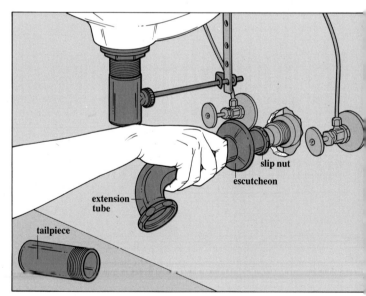

5 **Installing the drain extension.** Slide an escutcheon, slip nut and washer onto the drainpipe. Insert the pipe into the drain outlet protruding from the wall and tightly screw on the slip nut. Push the escutcheon against the wall. Wrap the threads of the drain tailpiece with plumbing-sealant tape and hand-tighten it into the drain T.

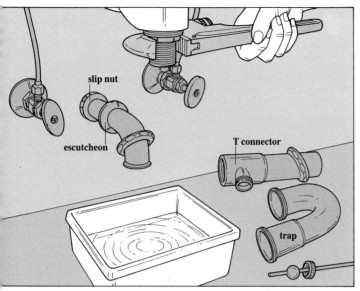

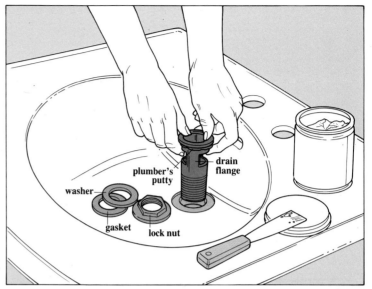

2 **Removing the old flange and fittings.** With a pipe wrench unscrew the drain T. Remove the lock nut and washer holding the drain fittings in the bottom of the washbasin *(above)*. Push the flange up and out through the hole in the basin. Pull out the drainpipe. If you have a two-piece swivel trap, there will be an elbow attachment to the drainpipe with a slip nut. Release the nut and elbow before removing the drainpipe.

3 **Sealing the drain flange.** Scrape off any old putty from around the drain opening, and clean and dry the surface of the washbasin. Roll a short rope of plumber's putty and press it under the edges of the flange of the new drain body *(above)*. Drop the drain body through the hole in the washbasin and press down the flange. Underneath the washbasin, push the gasket, then the washer, up over the bottom of the drain body. Then thread the lock nut up against the bottom of the washbasin, using a pipe wrench to tighten the nut.

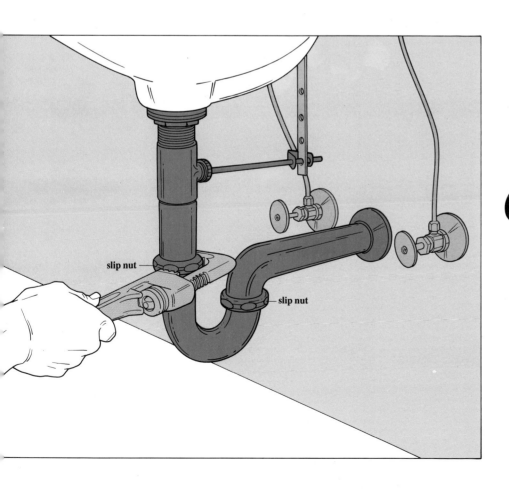

6 **Connecting the trap.** With slip nuts and washers in place on both the drain tailpiece and the drainpipe, align the trap with the tailpiece and the drainpipe. Loosely screw the two slip nuts. When all the sections are properly aligned, hand-tighten all of the nuts. Then make a final turn on each nut with a wrench *(left)*. Close the pop-up plug, fill the washbasin with water, then open the drain and check for leaks. Tighten slightly any joints that are leaking.

New Trim for Tub and Shower

Giving a new look to your bathtub, shower or toilet by changing the fittings may be easier than you think. Shower arms, tub spouts and drain overflow plates, for example, usually are standard interchangeable elements available wherever plumbing supplies are sold. Installing them is a matter of simply unscrewing the old and screwing in the new *(page 36)*. Toilet handles are no problem to replace, nor are toilet seats *(page 37, bottom)*.

Replacing a tub faucet, however, requires opening up the wall in which the faucet body and plumbing are located *(diagram, right)*. If your only concern is cosmetic, you can settle for a simpler change by leaving the faucet body intact and replacing only the surface fittings: the handles and their trim. Some faucet manufacturers sell new handles separately to fit onto their old faucets. Otherwise, you probably can use so-called universal replacements; these are sold in kits with adapters designed to fit the handles onto almost any two-handle or three-handle faucet *(opposite)*. Replacements with universal adapters come in several styles and such materials as polished brass, antiqued brass and chrome.

The tub or shower drain flange and pop-up or strainer are also not easily replaced. Fortunately, most old drain fittings are made of chrome-plated brass. You can remove them *(page 37, Steps 1 and 2)*, take them to a metal-finishing company, and have them replated to match your new tub trim.

A word of caution: Before stepping into the tub to work, pad it with towels or mats to protect the finish from being chipped or scratched by your shoes or by tools that you may accidentally drop. Cover the drain strainer to prevent screws and other small fittings from falling through it. And wrap adhesive tape around the jaws of pliers or wrenches to avoid damaging the finish on the fittings.

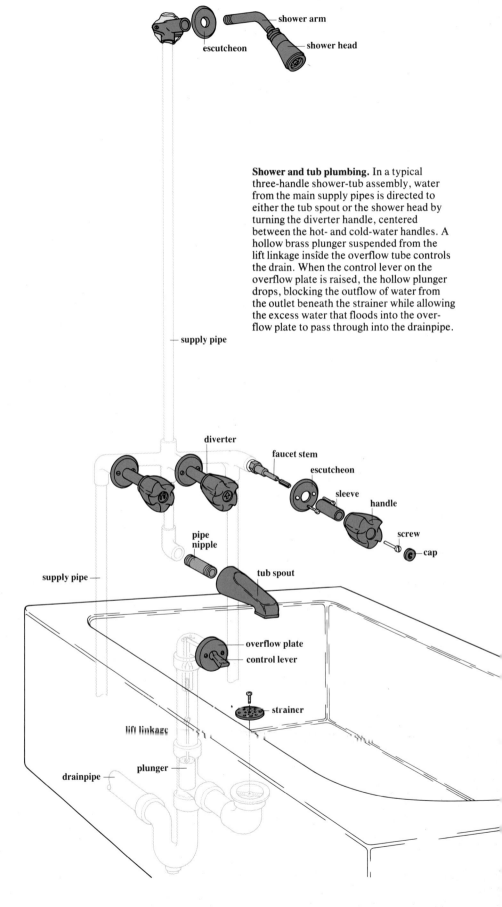

Shower and tub plumbing. In a typical three-handle shower-tub assembly, water from the main supply pipes is directed to either the tub spout or the shower head by turning the diverter handle, centered between the hot- and cold-water handles. A hollow brass plunger suspended from the lift linkage inside the overflow tube controls the drain. When the control lever on the overflow plate is raised, the hollow plunger drops, blocking the outflow of water from the outlet beneath the strainer while allowing the excess water that floods into the overflow plate to pass through into the drainpipe.

Revamping a Three-Handle Faucet

1 Removing the handles. Turn off the water supply to the tub. Pry off the cap in the center of each faucet handle with a thin screwdriver blade, or unscrew the cap with pliers if it has raised edges. Remove the screw holding the handle on the faucet stem and pull off the handle. If necessary, pry the handle off with a handle puller *(inset)*, available at plumbing-supply stores.

2 Removing escutcheons. Loosen the setscrew — if any — on the bottom edge of the escutcheon, or cover plate; remove the face screws, if any. Slide off the escutcheon. If the sleeve is a separate piece, as here, unscrew it counterclockwise with a tape-wrapped wrench *(above)*.

3 Marking holes. Center a new escutcheon over a faucet stem. Position the escutcheon so the hole for the setscrew is at the bottom and the holes for the face screws parallel the tub's edge. Mark the location of the face holes on the wall *(above)*. Then drill 1-inch-deep holes at the marks with a ¼-inch carbide bit. Insert the plastic screw anchors from the kit into the holes and attach the escutcheon with the screws.

4 Inserting the sleeves. Push a sleeve over a faucet stem and into the center of the escutcheon. Then measure the tip of the stem to make sure it protrudes at least ¾ inch beyond the sleeve *(above)*. If not, shorten the sleeve with a hacksaw and miter box.

5 Tightening the setscrews. Hold a sleeve firmly inside an escutcheon. Tighten the setscrew on the bottom edge of the escutcheon with a small screwdriver to anchor the sleeve securely over the faucet stem.

6 Attaching the handles. Fit one of the adapters *(inset)* from the replacement kit over the ridged top of each faucet stem. With the hex wrench from the kit tighten the three setscrews in the adapter *(above)*. Then put on the handles, securing each one with a screw; insert the screw through the washer if one is provided in the kit. Snap the handle caps in place.

Revamping a Single-Handle Faucet

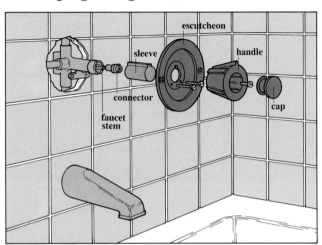

Separating the parts. To remove the old single-handle faucet, first pry off the cap concealing the screw that holds the handle to the connector, which fits on the stem inside the wall. Loosen the screw and pull the handle away from the stem. Lift off the connector. Remove the screws holding the escutcheon and pull it and the sleeve off the faucet body. To install new faucet trim, reverse the process — replacing the connector, fitting on the sleeve, screwing down the escutcheon, screwing on the handle and pressing on the cap.

Changing a Shower Head

Unscrewing the arm. Pull the shower-arm escutcheon away from the wall. Turning a pipe wrench counterclockwise, unscrew the shower arm and discard it with the shower head.

Wrap the threads on both ends of the new shower arm with plumbing-sealant tape. Screw the new head onto one end of the arm. Slide the new escutcheon over the other end. Hand-screw the free end of the arm into the pipe fitting. Using a clockwise motion (*above*), tighten the arm with a tape-wrapped wrench until the shower head points down. Press the escutcheon tightly against the wall.

Changing a Tub Spout

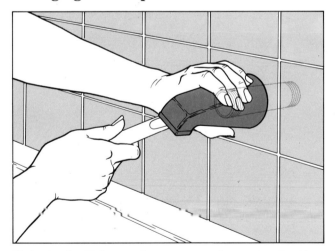

Fitting the pipe. To buy a replacement spout, first unscrew the old one by turning a pipe wrench in a counterclockwise direction. Take the old spout to the plumbing-supply store to be sure that the new spout you choose has a pipe nipple of the same length. Wrap the threads of the new pipe nipple with plumbing-sealant tape. Hand-tighten the new spout firmly into the wall fitting. Then, to provide extra leverage without damaging the finish, trim a stick of wood (*above*) to fit snugly inside the spout opening, and use the stick to help make the final turn that positions the spout opening down.

Changing an Overflow Plate

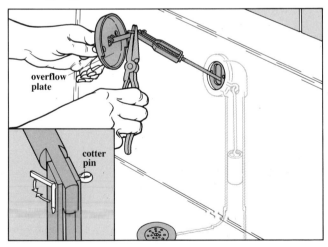

Handling a cotter pin. Loosen the two screws holding the overflow plate to the tub. With your hand, pull the plate and the attached mechanism out of the overflow hole far enough to reach the cotter pin (*inset*) that secures the mechanism to the back of the plate. With pliers, squeeze the ends of the cotter pin together and pull it out to free the plate. Use a new cotter pin to attach the new plate to the old mechanism. Ease the mechanism back into the overflow hole. Secure the new plate with the two screws provided.

Changing Drain Hardware

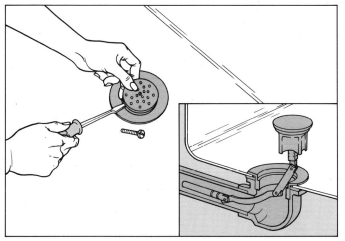

1 **Removing the strainer or plug.** Loosen the center screw that holds the drain strainer in place. Then lift out the screw and use the tip of the screwdriver to pry up the strainer *(above)*. Alternatively, pull the pop-up plug and its linkage *(inset)* out of the drain.

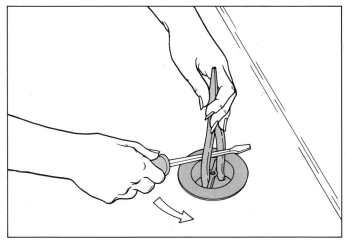

2 **Unscrewing the drain flange.** Slip the handles of a pair of pliers into the drain with one handle on each side of the drain's crossbar or, if there is no crossbar, against the projections on the wall of the drain. Wedge a screwdriver between the handles *(above)* and unscrew the drain flange in a counterclockwise direction. (If the pliers slip, you may need a special tool called a spud wrench.) The drain fittings are not standard replaceable parts, but you can have a metal-finishing company strip off the old chrome plating and either apply a clear protective finish to the brass bodies of the fittings or rechrome them.

Changing a Toilet Handle

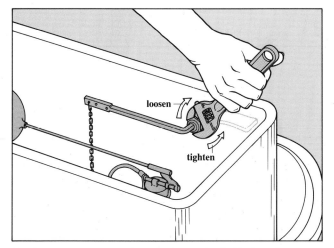

Manipulating the wrench. Remove the nut that holds the toilet handle in place by unscrewing it in a clockwise direction with an adjustable wrench; pull the old handle loose. Note: This nut is unscrewed in the opposite direction from that used for most nuts. Insert the new handle in the hole in the toilet tank and tighten the nut in a counterclockwise direction with the wrench.

Changing a Toilet Seat

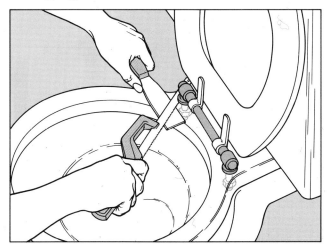

Dealing with the bolts. Spray the toilet-seat nuts on the underside of the bowl with penetrating lubricant several hours before removing the seat. Use a socket wrench to unscrew the nuts; lift off the seat. If the nuts do not unscrew, place a thin putty knife on the rim of the bowl next to the hinge to protect the china surface, and saw through the hinge bolts with a hacksaw *(above)*. Install a new seat by inserting the hinge bolts down through the holes in the bowl. Thread new nuts onto the bolts and hand-tighten them. Caution: Do not overtighten the bolts, lest you crack the bowl.

Installing a vanity

Installing a vanity in place of an old washbasin increases storage space for bathroom clutter while concealing unsightly plumbing pipes. And, as the name suggests, the vanity's bowl is bounded by generous counter space for cosmetics and toiletries.

Ready-made wood cabinets such as the one shown below can be found in widths ranging from 18 to 58 inches. Vitreous-china, simulated-granite or — as here — simulated-marble counters with built-in bowls come 20 to 96 inches wide. Assemblies vary, but the countertops usually overlap the cabinets by an inch or so at the front and sides. Cabinets and counters both appear in an array of styles, finishes and colors at kitchen and bath shops, furniture stores and home centers, and plumbing-supply stores.

Everyday tools — wrench, level, power drill and screwdriver — make quick work of installing a cabinet and countertop. However, if there is a baseboard, or tile or vinyl cove molding, where the vanity will stand, you will want to remove it to make the cabinet fit flush against the wall and you will need more tools: a pry bar, miter box, backsaw and hammer for wood; a utility knife for plastic.

Ceramic tile new enough to have been set in mastic can be removed with a pry bar and refitted later with a glass cutter. Old-fashioned tiles set in concrete cannot be lifted out. Instead, notch the base of the cabinet *(page 94, Step 2)*. To disconnect old plumbing and install new fittings, follow the instructions on pages 27-33.

Getting rid of the old washbasin is, of course, the first step. As shown at right, the technique you use depends on how the basin is attached to the wall or mounted on the pedestal. While removing a basin is not difficult, old fixtures are heavy and aging connections can break unexpectedly. You need a helper to hold the basin while you are underneath loosening pipes and brackets.

If you plan to tile, wallpaper, panel paint the bathroom, get that work done before you install the vanity so its edge will overlap the wall finish.

Even though few floors and walls are perfectly level or plumb, the vanity must be both so that water spilled on the countertop will run back into the bowl and the doors of the cabinet will close properly. Be prepared to level and plumb the cabinet with shims — tapered wood scraps or shingles — before attaching it to the wall.

Removing a Wall-hung Washbasin

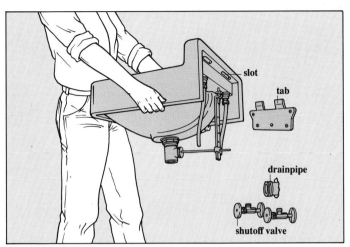

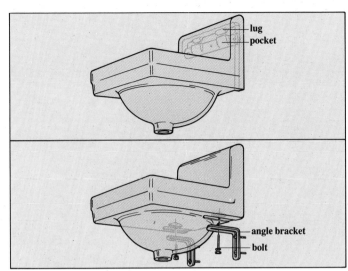

Lifting a washbasin off a bracket. Disconnect the water supply lines and the drain trap *(pages 27 and 32)*. Look underneath the basin to determine the kind of bracket securing it to the wall. For a basin hung on a tab-top bracket *(above, left)*, just lift the basin straight up. Remove the bracket and make any necessary wall repairs: Spackle holes in wallboard or plaster; put wood putty into paneling or wood wainscoting; replace damaged tiles. A washbasin hung from projecting lugs that fit into a bracket with pockets in the top *(right, top)* can also be lifted off.

But two bolts will secure a basin hung on angle brackets *(above)*. While a helper holds the washbasin, unscrew these bolts with an adjustable or open-end wrench. Remove the bolts. Then lift off the basin and detach the brackets from the wall.

Removing a Pedestal-Style Basin

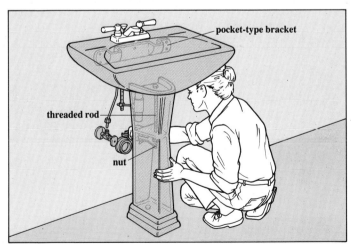

1 **Loosening the threaded rod.** Disconnect both water supply lines and the drain *(pages 27 and 32)*. Look inside the back of the hollow pedestal for the long threaded rod often — but not always — used to connect a basin to a pedestal. If you find a rod with an accessible nut on the end, use an adjustable or open-end wrench to loosen the nut. Then, following the directions above, lift the basin away from the pedestal and from the bracket on the wall. Remove the rod. If you are unable to reach the nut, you can loosen the base *(Step 2)* and remove basin and pedestal together.

2 **Removing the base.** Should you find a hold-down bolt or screw either inside the pedestal base or on the back edge of the base, remove the bolt or screw with a wrench or screwdriver. Lift the pedestal away. If you are unable to find a bolt, the pedestal probably is grouted to the floor. In this case, rock the pedestal back and forth until the base breaks loose. Remove the wall bracket that held the basin.

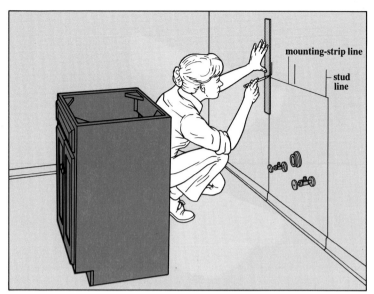

1 **Positioning the vanity.** Place the cabinet in the desired location so that the plumbing stub-outs will be roughly centered below the basin. Draw light pencil lines on the wall across the top of the cabinet's mounting strip and down both outside edges. Pull the cabinet away. For a wood-frame wall, locate the studs behind the cabinet (*page 124*) and, at each one, draw a short vertical line to the line marking the top of the mounting strip. To fit the cabinet flush against the wall, you can remove a mastic-set ceramic-tile baseboard by using a pry bar and hammer to gently pull out the two marked tiles and all those in between. If there is vinyl cove molding, use a straightedge and a utility knife to cut along the marked lines, then carefully peel away the center piece of molding.

2 **Removing a wood baseboard.** If you have a wood baseboard, first use a utility knife to break the paint seal at the top of the baseboard, working along the wall — and around a corner if need be — to a doorframe where the molding is cut at a 90° angle. Next to the door, tap a small pry bar into the seam behind the baseboard. Insert a smooth wood scrap behind the bar to increase your leverage and protect the wall. Pull the molding forward about an inch. Slip a shim behind the baseboard before removing the pry bar. Continue prying out the baseboard along the wall, or walls, to the corner beyond the vanity. Then return to the start and pry the baseboard completely free. Set the baseboard aside.

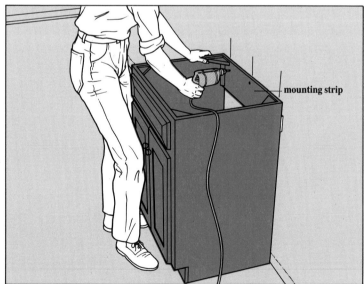

4 **Attaching the cabinet to the wall.** At the service panel, turn off the power to the bathroom and adjacent rooms. To attach a cabinet to studs in a painted or papered wallboard or plaster wall, drill %64-inch holes through the cabinet mounting strip ¾ inch from the top, and ¹⁄₁₆-inch holes at least 1 inch into the studs behind it. (Caution: If you strike a pipe, turn off the main water supply immediately and call a plumber.) Use 2¼-inch No. 6 self-tapping drywall screws to attach the cabinet to wood or metal studs. For a tiled or masonry wall, first drill %64-inch holes through the mounting strip. Mark the wall behind the cabinet. Pull the cabinet away, and use a ³⁄₁₆-inch carbide bit to drill holes 1⅛ inches deep into the tile or masonry for plastic anchors and 2-inch No. 6 screws.

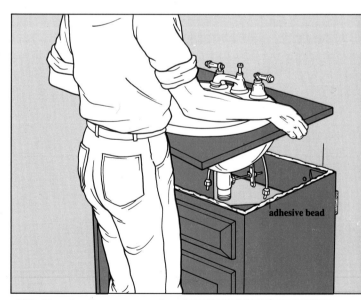

5 **Mounting the countertop.** Attach as many of the faucet and drain fittings (*pages 28-33*) to the countertop as is possible. Here, the handles, spout, water supply line, pop-up rod and drain assembly are in place. Run a bead of adhesive caulk around the cabinet's top edges, the press the countertop into the caulk. Wipe off any excess immediately.

3 **Leveling the vanity.** Put the cabinet back in position within its guidelines. Place a carpenter's level on the front top edge of the cabinet to check that the cabinet is level from side to side *(far left)*. If it is not, slide one or more shims under the cabinet until you have compensated for any unevenness of the floor.

Move the level to one side of the cabinet top and level it from front to back *(near left)*. Sand down slight irregularities on the wall; insert shims between the wall and cabinet to correct large irregularities.

After the vanity is level, draw a pencil line across every shim where it meets the cabinet. Remove one shim at a time, use a backsaw to cut it to the required length and slide the shim back in place.

shim

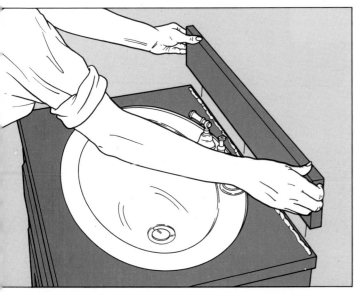

Attaching a backsplash. If the countertop has a separate backsplash, run a continuous bead of adhesive caulk along the back edge of the countertop. Then press the backsplash into the caulk and against the wall. Connect the water supply lines and the drain line *(pages 28-33)*. Turn on the electricity at the service panel.

7 **Finishing up.** To replace wood baseboard, use a backsaw to cut the baseboard at the pencil lines; reattach the end sections with fourpenny finishing nails. For tile, use a paste-type paint remover and razor to take off old mastic. Score each marked tile by pressing the wheel of a glass cutter along the pencil line; place the scored line face up over a pencil and push down both sides of the tile until it breaks. Reattach the cut tiles with tile mastic *(pages 81-82)*; when that has cured for 24 hours, grout the edges. To conceal shims where the floor and wall meet the vanity, finish decorative molding, such as quarter-round, to match the cabinet. Use a miter box and backsaw to angle the molding ends so they meet tightly at corners; attach the molding with fourpenny finishing nails *(above)*.

Converting a chest of drawers into a vanity

itted with a basin and fixtures, an old chest of drawers can become a handsome replacement for an ordinary washstand. A proper chest can make any bathroom harmonize with the décor of your home, while adding more useful storage space than most store-bought vanities.

Select a wall where stubbed-out plumbing lines *(Step 4)* are already in place, either newly installed or left by the removal of the old washbasin *(page 39)*. The chest is converted in three simple stages. First, openings are made in the chest top and back for the basin and plumbing. Then the chest is fastened to the wall and the plumbing is installed. The final stage is to modify drawers so they will close without colliding with the plumbing.

The chest can be virtually any style and any height that pleases the people who will use the washbasin. But one internal feature is essential: The rails that support the drawers must be at the sides of the chest *(opposite)*. Centrally located support rails would have to be cut away to make room for the plumbing. If the chest you plan to use has dust panels — sheets of thin plywood installed between drawers to seal them off from one another you will need to cut holes in some of the *(pages 48-49, Steps 1-4)*.

Select a chest before you choose a bsin. Measure the wall space to see whsize chest is most suitable. The basneed not be centered from side to sidethe chest, as it is here; allow your persoal taste to prevail, but situate thingsyou will not weaken the chest top whcutting the basin hole. Here, the basin iinches farther from the front edge thfrom the back, so that the chest's frorail — the horizontal board that suppothe front of the top — is only slighttrimmed when the basin hole is cut.

When shopping for a basin, keepmind that the dimensions given on tbox or in the catalogue may be either toverall dimensions of the basin or themensions of the hole you must cut to istall it. Ask your dealer for both setsmeasurements, and purchase a basin threquires a hole at least 4 inches smallfrom front to back than the chest top. Slect a basin that has holes in the rim fthe fittings so you do not have to maseparate holes for them in the chest to

You will need a saber saw withsmooth-cutting general-purpose bladepower drill with a ½-inch spade bit plassorted twist bits, and two cornclamps. For straight cuts, a table sawideal. Or you can combine a circular saor saber saw with a straightedge guidYou will also need a 1-by-3 board wiwhich to anchor the chest to the wallquarter sheet of ½-inch plywood, for tnew sections of the drawer backs; andfeet of ¾-inch quarter-round molding,serve as glue blocks.

Label the drawers — TOP, SECOND aso on — and remove them from the cheremove and set aside all hardware. Theto waterproof the chest top, cover itincluding the underside — with thrcoats of polyurethane varnish, sandiwith fine (150-grit) and very fine (220-grpaper before each coat and after the lcoat. Protect the rest of the chest and tdrawers, inside and out, with synthepenetrating oil, following the maker's drections. As you work on the chest, guaagainst scratching it. Pad the surfaceswhich you will lay the chest or its draers — an old blanket on the worktable wdo the job — and cover the shoe plateyour saber saw with masking tape.

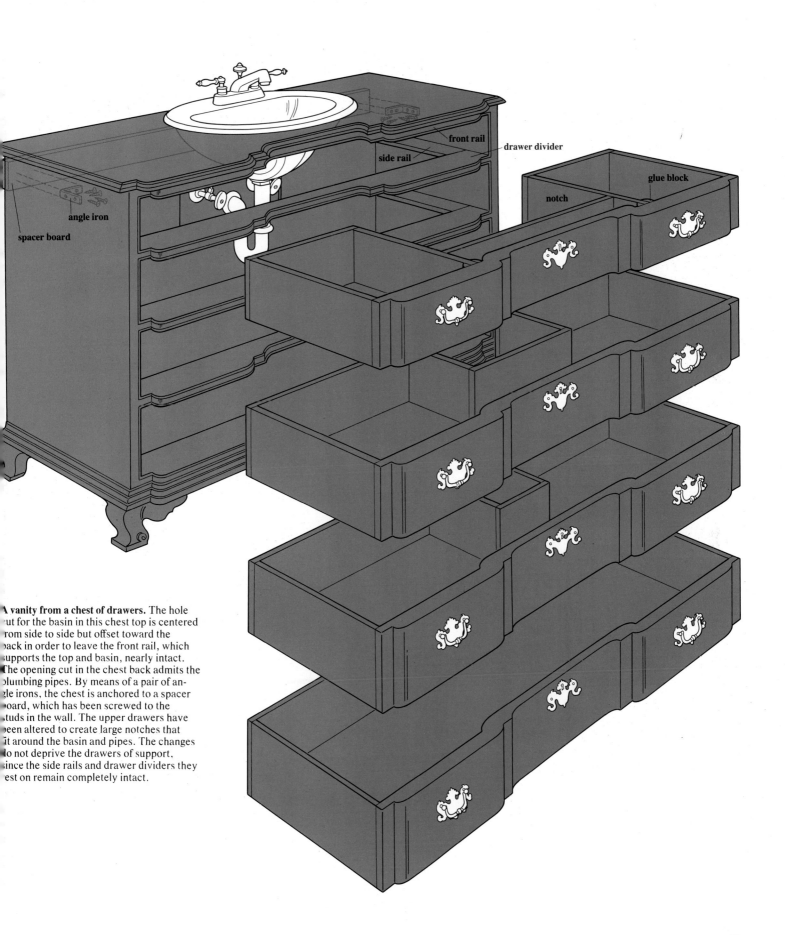

A vanity from a chest of drawers. The hole cut for the basin in this chest top is centered from side to side but offset toward the back in order to leave the front rail, which supports the top and basin, nearly intact. The opening cut in the chest back admits the plumbing pipes. By means of a pair of angle irons, the chest is anchored to a spacer board, which has been screwed to the studs in the wall. The upper drawers have been altered to create large notches that fit around the basin and pipes. The changes do not deprive the drawers of support, since the side rails and drawer dividers they rest on remain completely intact.

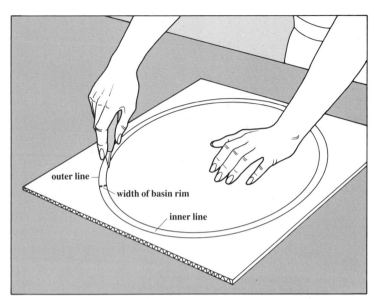

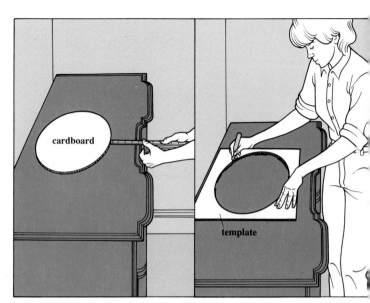

1 **Making a template for the basin opening.** Place the basin upside down on a piece of heavy cardboard and trace it. Measure the width of the underside of the basin's rim. On the cardboard, draw a second line, which lies inside the first by a distance equal to the width of the rim: This inner line describes the hole to be cut in the chest top for the basin. Cut the cardboard along the inner line with a utility knife *(above)*. Save the piece you remove, for use in Step 2. Check the template for size by fitting it onto the upside-down basin. The template should move easily down around the bowl to the rim; if necessary, trim it to fit.

2 **Cutting the basin opening.** Lay the cardboard piece cut from the middle of the template on the chest and measure from all edges of the chest top to position the cardboard where the basin should be *(above, left)*. With a fine felt-tipped marker, outline the cardboard with a dashed line, then remove it. Now center the template around this outline and draw a solid line along the inner edge of the template *(above, right)*. Remove the template and drill a starter hole just inside the solid line, using a ½-inch spade bit in a power drill. Then cut along the line with a saber saw. As you near the end of the cut, have a helper hold the cutout wood in place to prevent its falling and leaving a splintered edge. Seal the cut edges with three coats of polyurethane varnish.

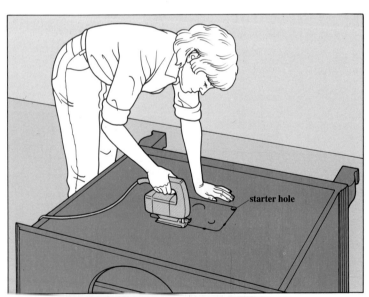

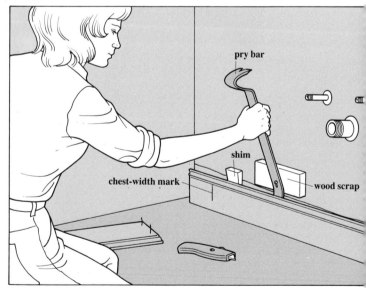

5 **Cutting an opening for the plumbing.** Drill a starter hole just inside the rectangle, as you did in Step 2; then cut out the rectangle with a saber saw. (If your chest has dust panels, use the techniques shown on pages 48-49 to complete the chest-back cutout and alter the panels.)

Stand the chest in front of the stub-outs and push it into place against the wall. Near each top rear corner of the chest, make pencil marks on the wall to show the chest's height and width. Then measure the distance between the wall and the top of the chest back. If this distance is ¾ inch or less, go on to Step 7. If the distance is greater than ¾ inch, you will need to remove the baseboard from the wall behind the chest, as shown in Step 6.

6 **Removing baseboard from behind the chest.** Mark the chest width on the baseboard, then move the chest aside. If, as here, the piece of baseboard you want to remove is trapped in place by adjacent pieces, start removing baseboard where the end of a piece is not blocked, such as next to a doorway, and work around to the washbasin wall. Break the paint seal between baseboard and wall with a utility knife. Pry the baseboard away with a pry bar, protecting the wall with a scrap of wood and inserting shims behind the loosened baseboard as you go. When you have removed the basin-wall piece, saw through it at the chest-width marks and discard the middle section. Nail the two endpieces, plus any other pieces you removed, back in place with fourpenny finishing nails.

3 **Marking the top drawer for the notch.** Place a pad of folded newspaper on each side of the basin cutout, and stand the top drawer on its back atop the pads. Center the drawer from side to side, and align it so its back bottom edge crosses the widest part of the basin cutout. Make pencil marks at the two points on the drawer's edge where it intersects the sides of the cutout. Turn the drawer onto its face on a padded surface and use a carpenter's square to draw two parallel lines, perpendicular to the bottom rear edge, across the back of the drawer. Then turn the drawer upside down and continue the lines — still perpendicular to the rear edge — across the drawer's bottom (*inset*). Set the drawer aside.

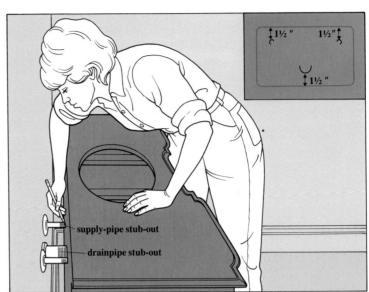

4 **Marking the chest back.** Center the chest in the space it is to occupy and push it toward the wall until its back touches the short pipes, or stubouts, that protrude from the wall. Reach down into the space between chest and wall, and pencil the pipe locations on the chest back, outlining the top and outer sides of each supply pipe and the underside of the drainpipe. Move the chest away from the wall and lay it face down on a well-padded surface. Make pencil marks 1½ inches above and 1½ inches to the outside of both supply-pipe outlines and another mark 1½ inches below the drainpipe outline. Now draw a round-cornered rectangle whose sides connect the pencil marks (*inset*).

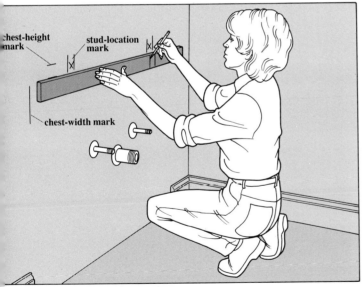

7 **Mounting the spacer board.** Measure the width of the chest back inside the chest; cut a 1-by-3 board to this length, and stain its ends and one edge to match the chest. Find and mark the stud locations (*page 124*) between chest-width marks. Center the spacer between the chest-width marks, and pencil the stud locations on it (*above*). Drill two counterbored ³⁄₁₆-inch holes through the board at each stud location. Position the board on the wall 2 inches below the chest-height marks and stick an awl through the holes to mark screw positions. At those marks, drill ⅛-inch pilot holes 1 inch deep into the studs. Mount the board with 2-inch No. 10 screws. On masonry, or on wallboard where studs are not conveniently located, use other appropriate fasteners (*pages 124-125*).

8 **Mounting the angle irons.** Slide the chest into place. In each inside back corner, position a 2½-inch angle iron, or corner brace, 2 inches below the chest top, and mark the screw holes. Drill ⅛-inch pilot holes ⅝ inch deep at the marks on the side (or side framing member) of the chest. At the marks on the chest back, drill ¼-inch shank holes through the back and ⅛-inch pilot holes ⅝ inch deep into the spacer board. Secure the angle irons with ⅝-inch No. 8 screws driven into the sides and 1¼-inch No. 8 screws driven through the back into the spacer. Now squeeze a bead of silicone sealant all the way around the underside of the basin rim. Set the basin in the hole and use a wet finger to wipe away excess sealant. Connect all the plumbing (*pages 28-33*). ▶

45

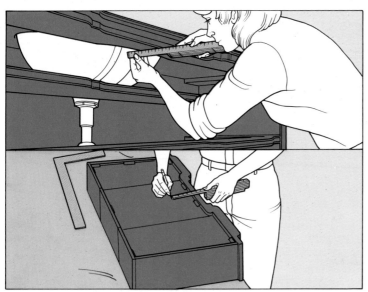

9 **Completing the notch outline.** Measure from the front of the basin to the front of the chest's drawer opening *(top picture, above)*. Measure the same distance across the drawer bottom from the front edge toward the back and make a mark *(lower picture)*. Using the carpenter's square, draw a line through this point to connect the two parallel lines, completing the outline of the notch.

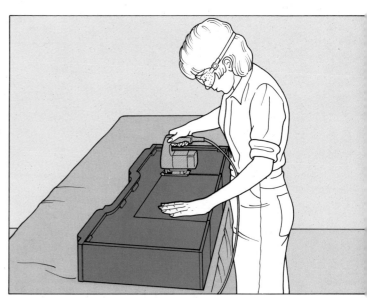

10 **Cutting out the notch.** Stand the drawer on its front on the worktable. Steadying the drawer with one hand, start cutting with a saber saw at the edge of the drawer's back. Following the notch outline, saw across the back; stop an inch from the drawer bottom. Saw the other side of the notch the same way. Turn the drawer upside down and continue the cuts into and across the bottom *(above)*. Do not bother squaring the corners of the notch; just round them in tight curves with the saw. If the back and bottom start coming apart as you cut the notch, secure them with fourpenny finishing nails, blunted by a light hammer blow on the tip to make them less likely to split the wood than sharp nails would be.

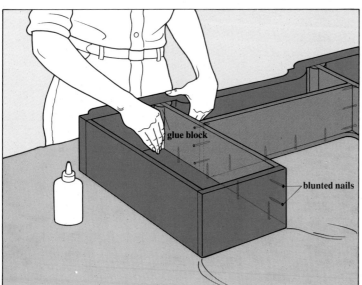

glue block

blunted nails

13 **Installing the frame.** Fit the assembly into the drawer. Stand the drawer on its front on padding and drive two blunted fourpenny finishing nails through the drawer back into each sidepiece. Turn the drawer upside down and drive nails through the drawer bottom into the edges of all three frame pieces at 4-inch intervals. Turn the drawer right side up and secure the front ends of the sidepieces with glue blocks: Cut four pieces of ¾-inch quarter-round molding to the frame height; spread yellow glue on the two flat sides of a block, then press it into place *(above)*. After installing all four blocks, let the glue dry for two hours. Cover the exposed plywood edges with iron-on veneer banding, and stain all new wood.

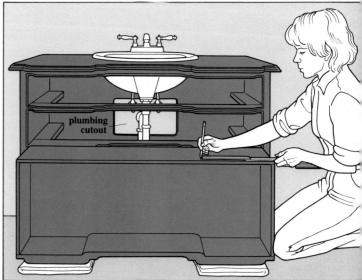

plumbing cutout

14 **Marking the sides of the second-drawer notch.** Stand the second drawer on its front on padding in front of the chest. Reach into the chest and measure horizontally from the right-hand rear corner (or from the inner edge of the side rail's drawer guide, if there is one) to the nearer side of the plumbing cutout. Subtract ½ inch for clearance and transfer this measurement to the drawer's back, measuring from the right-hand side toward the center of the drawer *(above)*. Repeat for the left-hand side of the chest and the drawer. Use a carpenter's square to draw lines from the pencil marks down the back of the drawer and across the bottom.

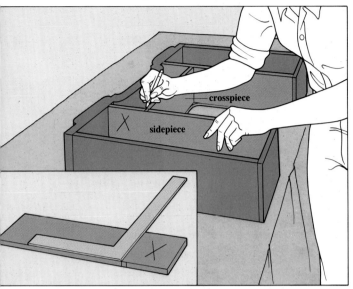

11 **Cutting notch framing.** Measure inside the drawer from front to back, then measure the height of the drawer back. Cut two sidepieces to these dimensions from ½-inch plywood. Measure the width of the notch. Use this dimension and the height of the drawer back to cut a ½-inch plywood crosspiece. Stand the three pieces in the drawer, along the notch edges. Pencil an X on the outer side of each sidepiece. Pencil two lines across the top edge of each sidepiece where the crosspiece meets it *(above)*. Remove the pieces from the drawer. Use a carpenter's square to extend the crosspiece marks as two parallel lines across the outer (X-marked) surface of each sidepiece, perpendicular to the top edge *(inset)*.

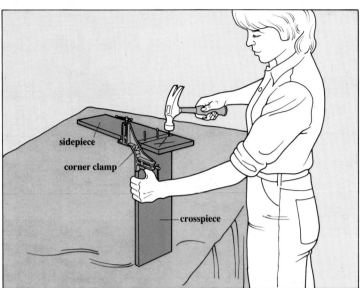

12 **Assembling the frame.** Lay one sidepiece on a worktable with the outer, X-marked surface up. Start three blunted fourpenny finishing nails between the parallel pencil lines, spacing them evenly; do not drive them all the way through the wood. Arrange the crosspiece and one sidepiece in a T shape in a corner clamp, aligning the partly driven nails over one end of the crosspiece. Stand the crosspiece on its other end, as shown above, and drive in the three nails. Repeat this procedure with the other sidepiece to complete the H-shaped assembly. Sand away the pencil marks.

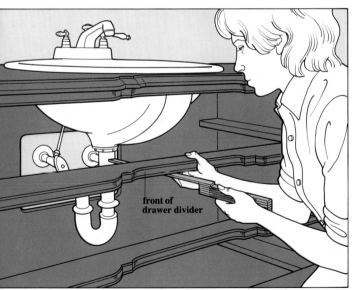

15 **Marking the front of the notch.** Hold a ruler horizontally under the drawer divider at the top of the second drawer opening *(above)*. Measure from the front of the drainpipe (or the front of the basin, if the basin extends that low) to the front of the drawer divider. Subtract 1 inch for clearance and transfer this measurement to the corresponding position on the drawer bottom, measuring from the front toward the back. Use a carpenter's square to complete the notch outline, as you did in Step 9; cut it out with a saber saw.

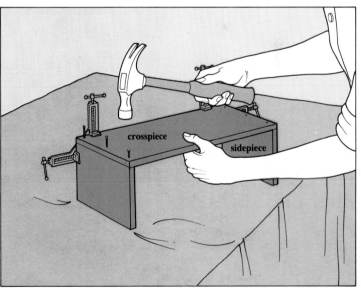

16 **Making the second-drawer notch frame.** Measure the notch from front to back; then measure the drawer-back height. Cut two sidepieces to these dimensions from ½-inch plywood. Cut a crosspiece that is the height of the drawer's back and is 1 inch longer than the drawer notch is wide. Start three blunted fourpenny finishing nails evenly spaced in a row ¼ inch from each end of the crosspiece. Secure the three pieces with two corner clamps, as shown above, aligning the sidepieces under the nails in the crosspiece. Drive the nails home, then sand the U-shaped assembly. ▶

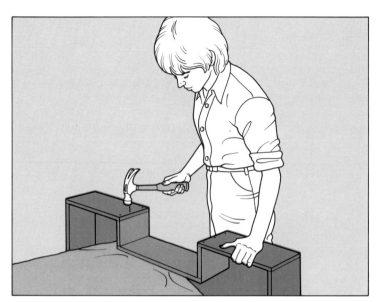

17 **Installing the notch frame.** Place the U-shaped assembly, cross-piece down, on one corner of a worktable, and rest the drawer on it as shown above. (If the old back pieces start coming loose, tack them in place with blunted nails and prop up the whole drawer from below while installing the notch frame.) Secure the frame by driving three blunted fourpenny finishing nails through each cut end of the old drawer back and into the new sidepieces (*above*). Now set the drawer upside down on the table and drive blunted nails at 4-inch intervals through the drawer bottom and into the notch frame. Turn the drawer upright, apply veneer banding to the exposed plywood edges, and stain the new wood to match the old.

18 **Notching the third drawer.** Slide the third drawer gently into the chest. If the drawer back clears the P trap, you need not alter this drawer. If it hits the trap, notch the drawer in the following way: Reach in through the second-drawer opening with ruler and pencil and make marks on the top edge of the drawer back, 1 inch from each side of the trap. Remove the drawer. On the outside bottom of the second drawer, measure from the front of the drawer to the front of the notch; mark this distance on the third drawer. Outline the notch and cut the drawer as in Steps 9 and 10; then cut, assemble and install the notch frame as in Steps 16 and 17. Remount all the drawer hardware and replace the drawers in the chest.

Dealing with Dust Panels

Dust panels are useful horizontal partitions that keep dust from drifting into the drawers below. In a chest being converted to a vanity, however, some of these panels will prove to be obstacles that must be cut to make room for the basin and the plumbing. These changes should be made after the basin hole has been cut and the cutout for the pipes has been outlined on the chest back (*pages 44-45, Steps 1-4*).

Thin plywood dust panels are held in place by frames inside the chest. Although the panels themselves do not reinforce the chest's structure, the frames do, and so should be altered as little as possible. You will have to cut the frame of any panel that crosses the plumbing cutout. But for openings in other panels, draw and cut close to the back frame without cutting through it.

When you have made all of the necessary alterations to the dust panels (*opposite, bottom right*), continue with Step 5 on page 44.

3 **Cutting the dust panel.** Stand the chest upright, then use a carpenter's square to draw, on the panel, a line that is perpendicular to the chest back and that extends from each saw cut to a point 4 inches from the front of the chest. Draw a third line connecting the front ends of the first two, and drill a starter hole in the outline (if the dust panels are very close together, you may have to angle the drill). Cut along the lines with a saber saw and remove the scrap.

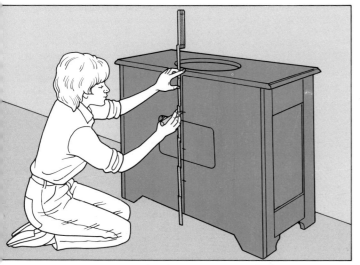

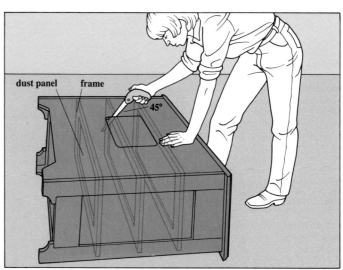

Marking dust-panel locations. On the chest's back, draw a vertical line that crosses the outline for the plumbing cutout *(page 45, Step 4)*. Working at the front of the upright chest, measure the distance from each dust panel to the floor. Transfer these measurements to the vertical line on the chest back, marking across the line for each panel. If any panel mark falls within the outline for the plumbing cutout, use a level to draw a horizontal line through the mark and across both sides of the outline.

2 **Sawing out the plumbing cutout.** Drill a starter hole on the outline on the chest back. Use a saber saw to cut along the outline to a point 2 inches from a dust-panel mark. Then, to avoid damaging the saber saw, switch to a compass, or keyhole, saw — a small handsaw — to cut the part of the outline that intersects the panel. Keep the saw at a 45° angle to the chest back *(above)* so that it also cuts down through the panel frame and part of the dust panel. At a point 2 inches beyond the panel mark, switch back to the saber saw. Use the handsaw again at the panel mark on the other side of the outline.

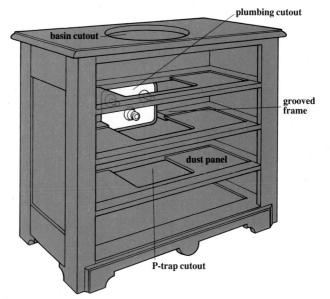

Marking and cutting other panels. Any dust panels between the plumbing cutout and the chest top must also be cut. On the underside of the chest top, measure from the left chest wall to the left side of the basin cutout, and transfer this measurement to the nearest panel *(above)*. Repeat for the right side and for the front of the basin cutout. Draw a rectangular outline connecting these three marks and cut the hole, leaving the frame intact. If there is a panel less than 4 inches below the bottom of the chest-back cutout, transfer to it the dimensions of the first dust-panel cutout *(Step 3)*. Again leaving the frame intact, cut that hole.

5 **The completed alterations.** In the dust-paneled chest above, the top, back and panels have been cut to admit the basin and the plumbing. The opening in the lowest dust panel makes room for the drain's P trap. The chest is now ready to be anchored to the wall *(pages 44-45, Steps 5-8)*. To complete the conversion, install the basin and plumbing *(page 45, Step 8)*, and alter the drawers *(pages 46-48, Steps 9-18)*.

A Sink in a Side Table

Installing a basin and faucet in a traditional side table, as shown at right, creates a fully plumbed version of an old-fashioned washstand. A basin with a solid rim and a wide-spread faucet will underscore the period look.

Any wood table about 2 feet deep and 3 feet wide with stationary legs and top can serve; a gate-leg or drop-leaf table will not do. Outline the part of the table-top within the aprons — the sidepieces that support it — with masking tape (*Step 1*) to determine what size basin and faucet it can accommodate and how they can be arranged. For comfortable use of the faucet handles, allow at least 1½ inches between backsplash and handles. When choosing a basin, ask your dealer for overall dimensions as well as the dimensions of the cutout required for installation.

The first step in shaping the table is to saw off all but ¾ inch — the thickness of a 1-by-3 — from the overhang at the back. When you are ready to install the table, attach a spacer board of matching length to that apron, and screw the apron and spacer together to the wall.

If the piece of overhang you have removed is at least 1½ inches wide, use it for the backsplash. Otherwise, take it to a lumberyard and buy wood of the same kind, ¾ inch thick, 1½ or 2 inches wide and as long as the table.

The ends of the spacer and all surfaces of the backsplash, if you buy a new one, should be stained to match the table. You may also want to distress — intentionally damage — new backsplash wood to make it look worn. Round its sharp edges with a file and, if the table is dented or scratched, mar the new wood with a ball-peen hammer or a tenpenny common nail. Sand the distressed wood with medium (100-grit), fine (150-grit) and then very fine (220-grit) sandpaper before staining it.

The tools required include a handsaw, saber saw, power drill and screwdriver. Before using the saber saw, cover its shoe plate with masking tape to prevent its marring the tabletop. When you have completed Step 6 (*opposite*), install the basin and faucet (*page 45, Step 8*).

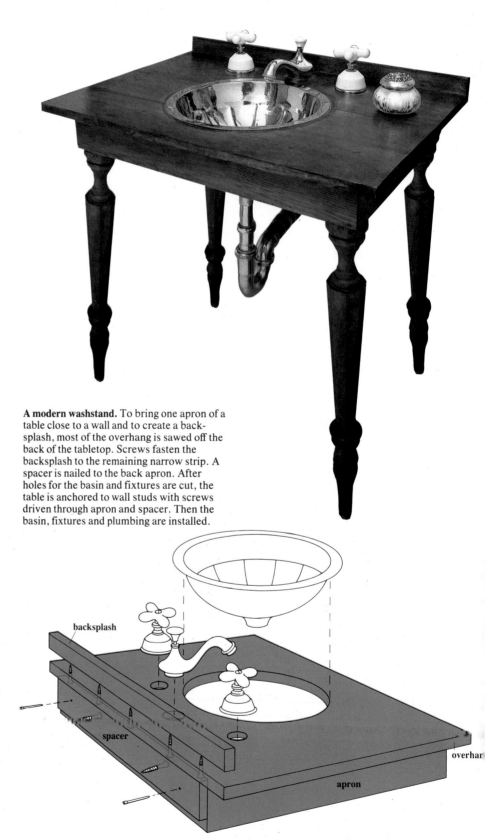

A modern washstand. To bring one apron of a table close to a wall and to create a backsplash, most of the overhang is sawed off the back of the tabletop. Screws fasten the backsplash to the remaining narrow strip. A spacer is nailed to the back apron. After holes for the basin and fixtures are cut, the table is anchored to wall studs with screws driven through apron and spacer. Then the basin, fixtures and plumbing are installed.

backsplash

spacer

overhang

apron

Drilling and cutting the top. Measure the overhangs and mark the apron locations on the tabletop with strips of masking tape. Make templates of the faucet and handle bases and of the basin *(page 44, Step 1)*. Arrange the templates on the table and use an awl to mark the centers of the fixture templates *(above)* and the perimeter of the basin template. Drill holes for the fixtures, using a 1⅛-inch spade bit. Make the basin cutout *(page 44, Step 2)*.

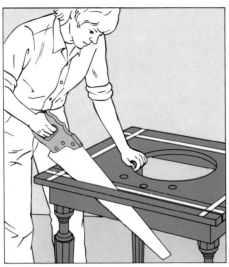

2 Trimming the top. Subtract ¾ inch from the width of the overhang on the side of the table that will abut the wall; with a pencil, draw a cutting line at this distance from the table's edge. Saw along the line with a handsaw *(above)*. Push the table into place and make pencil marks on the wall to indicate the top and sides of the tabletop and the bottom and sides of the apron.

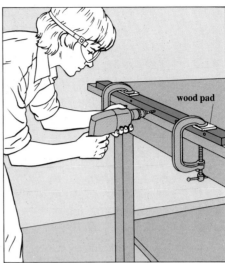

3 Making the backsplash. If the strip cut from the tabletop is at least 1½ inches wide, clamp it to a worktable. Otherwise, substitute a newly finished ¾-by-1½-inch strip of wood that is the length of the table's edge. Pad the clamps with wood scraps and position the strip with a narrow side — the cut side if it came from the table — toward you. With a ³⁄₃₂-inch twist bit, drill a row of holes 1 inch deep and 6 inches apart into the side facing you *(above)*.

4 Mounting the backsplash. Pull off the tape from the tabletop's cut side. Lay the backsplash half its own thickness from the cut table edge, drilled side facing out and ends aligned with the table sides. At each drilled hole, mark and drill a ³⁄₁₆-inch hole through the tabletop. Spread clear silicone sealant on the drilled side of the backsplash, stand it upright and fasten it with 1½-inch No. 8 wood screws. Wipe away excess sealant.

5 Making and mounting the spacer. Cut a 1-by-3 board to the length of the apron beneath the backsplash. Stain the board's ends to match the table. Hold the spacer against the apron with its upper side against the overhang and fasten it in place with two fourpenny finishing nails. Waterproof the tabletop *(page 42)*.

6 Anchoring the table. Find and mark the studs *(page 124)* between the apron-width marks on the wall. Place the table against the wall. Two inches below the underside of the tabletop, at two stud locations, drill a ¼-inch hole through the apron and spacer *(above)*. Then drill a ⅛-inch hole 1½ inches deep into each stud. Secure the table with 3-inch-long No. 10 wood screws. Install the plumbing *(page 45, Step 8)*.

51

Transforming walls and floors

When you set out to unify the look of a bath-room, you encounter special challenges and opportunities. You want walls and floors that are cleanable but not drab, lighting that is bright but not glaring; you must always consider the presence of water and vapor. On the other hand, you can choose from among products not generally used elsewhere in the house. This chapter presents several: incandescent tubes to illumine a make-up/shaving center *(pages 60-63);* a hanging soffit to suffuse a bathroom with light *(pages 64-67);* paints applied to make walls look like marble *(pages 68-75);* ceramic tiles *(pages 78-87)* or washable carpet *(pages 76-77).* In addition, the following pages explain how to install the one decoration everyone wants in a bathroom — a glass mirror *(below)* or a plastic one *(page 55).*

Plastic mirror can be easily cut into imaginative orna-mental shapes, but glass is optically superior and gives a truer reflection. So, for the mirror over the washbasin, use fine ¼-inch glass mirror and have the dealer cut it. In determining the mirror's dimensions, leave at least ⅛ inch of clear wall space all around it, to ease installation and to allow for later settling of the building. Never set a mirror directly atop a backsplash; water could creep onto the reflective backing, which is fragile and needs to stay dry.

For the same reason, any mirror should be mounted with about ⅛-inch space behind it, to permit air circulation. Support glass mirror with special hardware: J clips to hold the bottom ⅛ inch out from the wall and L clips to keep the top steady *(Steps 2 and 4).* Also get from your mirror dealer small self-adhesive felt pads to serve as spacers between mirror and wall and to prevent the J clips from scratching the backing. For permanence in areas subject to earth-quakes, you can supplement the clips with an adhesive called mirror mastic *(box, page 54)* in place of the pads.

Freshly plastered or painted walls give off fumes that can corrode mirror backing; let such a wall dry for a week before installing a mirror. The backing is even susceptible to the salts and oils on human skin; wear gloves to handle mirror. To clean a mirror, dissolve mild soap in warm water, moisten a soft cloth with the suds and apply them sparingly; avoid ammonia, which can damage the backing. Polish with a dry cloth and dry the edges thoroughly.

How to Carry a Glass Mirror

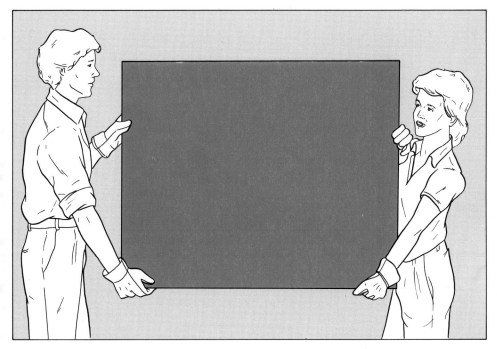

Glass mirror is heavy as well as fragile: One square foot of ¼-inch mirror weighs a bit more than 3 pounds. The largest size you should handle yourself is 12 square feet — for example, 3 feet by 4, or 6 by 2.

The mirror you buy will probably be wrapped in paper. When you get it home, bring it indoors, unwrap it to let it adjust to your home's humidity, and store it on edge.

Glass mirror — like all glass — should be carried on edge so that it cannot sag and break of its own weight. To protect the mirror and your hands, wear work gloves while carrying it. On stairs, keep the stronger person at the lower end, supporting more of the weight.

If a mirror does begin to fall, the only thing to do is what the professionals do — get out of the way. *Never* try to catch a mirror.

Installing a Glass Mirror

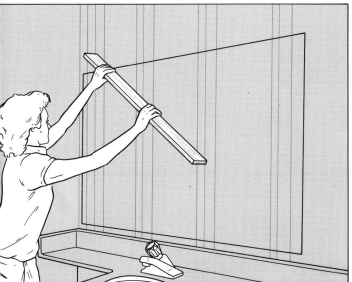

Checking the wall for high spots. Measuring at least ⅛ inch up from the backsplash and in from adjacent walls, lightly pencil tick marks on the wall for the mirror's bottom corners. Using a straightedge, draw a base line between the marks. Then run the edge of a long, straight board over the wall to locate high spots. (The factory edge of a length of plywood works well.) Check the height of any bulge by centering your straightedge board on the bulge and holding one end against the wall, then having your helper measure the gap between wall and board at the other end and halving this distance. A bulge of more than ⅛ inch must be sanded down with coarse (60-grit), then fine (150-grit), sandpaper. If you repaint the sanded area, wait a week before installing the mirror.

2 **Mounting the J clips.** Find and mark the studs *(page 124)* inside the mirror base-line area. Hold a J clip with its back bottom corner on the base line in front of the stud nearest one end of the line. Make a pencil mark through each hole in the clip; drill ³⁄₃₂-inch holes 1½ inches deep into the stud at each mark. Fasten the clip with 1½-inch No. 6 flat-head screws, and cover each clip with a self-adhesive felt pad *(inset)*. Mount another J clip on the stud closest to the other end of the base line. If the mirror is wider than 60 inches, mount a J clip on every second intervening stud. If your wall lacks studs, or if they are not suitably placed, use the appropriate alternative fasteners *(pages 124-125)* for the clips. ▶

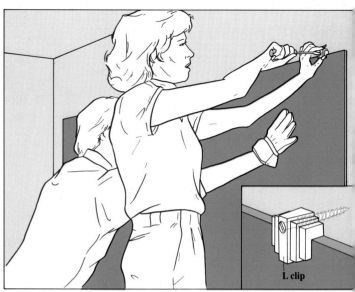

L clip

3 **Placing mirror in J clips.** Using a level to make sure the yardstick is vertical, measure up the wall from the base line at each J clip a distance equal to the height of the mirror plus ¼ inch. Mark and drill a ³⁄₃₂-inch hole 1½ inches deep into the stud for each L clip that will secure the top of the mirror. Stick rows of two or three self-adhesive felt pads on the back of the mirror, several inches from each side. With a helper, lift up the mirror in front of the wall, keeping its face forward. Lower the bottom edge of the mirror into the J clips, but hold the top edge tilted forward *(above)*. Slide the mirror sideways into its intended position, leaving at least ⅛ inch between the mirror's edge and an adjacent wall.

4 **Mounting the L clips.** Slowly push the top of the mirror back until the felt pads are against the wall. Listen to the sound the mirror makes as it comes to rest. If the sound is clear, not muted, some part of the mirror is striking the wall. Lean the top of the mirror away from the wall a few inches, reach behind it and put more felt pads atop the first ones. Test the sound again and add more pads if necessary. Then, while your help holds the mirror upright, mount an L clip *(inset)* at each drilled hole at the top of the mirror. Use 1½-inch No. 6 round-head screws and tighten them just enough for security, not enough to bow the mirror.

How to Use Mastic Adhesive

Mirror mastic is a special type of glue that will help secure a mirror to the wall without damaging the backing. It is particularly useful in earthquake zones because it remains resilient and will flex with tremors. But mastic is messy to use and is permanent. Attempting to remove a mirror glued with mastic usually damages both mirror and wall.

If you use mastic, be sure to read the directions; some brands require preparation of the mirror backing. Proceed as in Steps 1 and 2 on page 53. Then lay the mirror face down on a clean blanket. Using a wood scrap to avoid scratching the backing, apply four pats of mastic — each about 1½ inches square and ¾ inch thick — to every square foot of mirror. Keep the mastic 2½ inches from the edges. Install the mirror as above, but omit the felt pads; the mastic will serve the same purpose.

A mirror that is easy to cut

For a delightfully decorative mirror, such as the imitation Palladian window below, acrylic has several advantages over glass. If you drop acrylic mirror, it is unlikely to break. You can cut it into almost any shape with a saber saw. It is light in weight and can be safely mounted with double-faced plastic foam tape. The distortions in acrylic's reflections are acceptable in small pieces like these; and the ease of working with acrylic may make its premium cost well worthwhile.

Take careful measurements of your wall, and make a scale drawing of it on graph paper, including any fixtures, such as the toilet-paper holder seen here. Use this drawing to plan the size and location of your mirror design. Mark the boundaries of your design on the wall (Step 1), with drafting tape or some other low-tack (less sticky) tape, which will peel off the wall without damaging paint or wallpaper.

The window design shown here is made of ⅛-inch mirror, and the foam tape is ¹⁄₁₆ inch thick and 1 inch wide. Mirror that is ¼ inch thick will stay flatter and thus have less distortion, but it will require more of the mounting tape. Ask your dealer to recommend the correct amount of foam tape for your job; the tape is available in rolls, in a variety of lengths and widths.

The mirror comes in 4-foot-by-8-foot sheets. For a fee, your supplier will cut all of the pieces, if you provide measurements for the rectangular pieces and templates for the curved ones. If you cut the pieces yourself, be sure to do so in a well-ventilated area; the plastic can give off fumes when cut. Equip your saber saw with a blade whose teeth are widely set; such a blade cuts a wide path, or kerf, and keeps the plastic from fusing to the blade.

The spaces between panes in the design shown here are all ½ inch wide. Mounting the mirrors uniformly at that distance is simplified by using two ½-inch-thick pieces of parting bead cut 18 inches long as spacers.

As you work with acrylic mirror, leave the protective covering — paper or plastic — on the face until you are finished handling and mounting the mirror. When the mirror needs to be cleaned, use only mild soap and water and a soft cloth; paper towels can scratch it. If scratches do appear, occasional polishing with automobile paste wax will hide them. Plastic mirror, like glass mirror, should be dried carefully after being washed, because even plain water that "puddles" — gathers along the bottom edge of the mirror — can attack the backing and cause unsightly stains to develop.

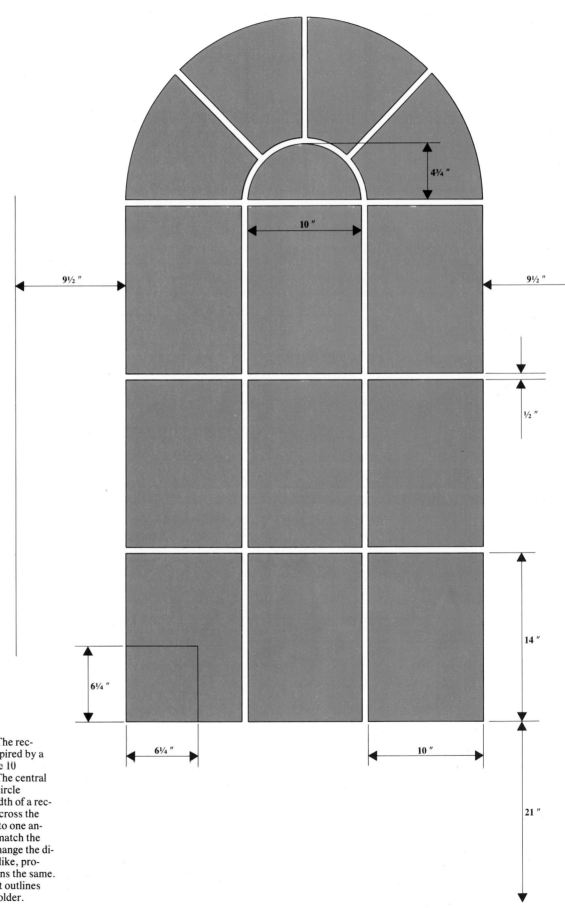

An illusory window of mirrors. The rectangular panes in this design inspired by a classic 16th Century window are 10 inches wide by 14 inches high. The central curved pane is based on a semicircle whose diameter matches the width of a rectangle. The four curved panes across the top of the window are identical to one another; their straight sides, too, match the width of a rectangle. You can change the dimensions of this pattern as you like, providing you keep these proportions the same. The 6¼-inch square at lower left outlines the cutout for the toilet-paper holder.

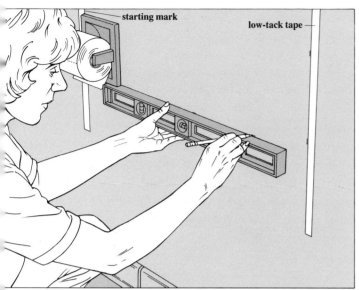

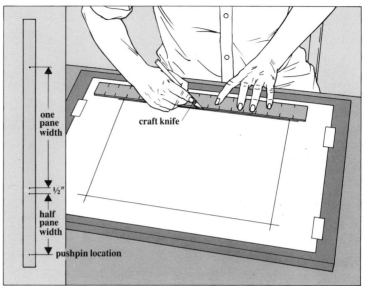

1 Outlining the mirror area. On graph paper, draw the wall where the mirror will go; then outline the design to scale on the paper. On the wall, make a mark for the left-hand boundary, by measuring from the wall's left edge or by beginning at whatever fixture your design includes — here, a toilet-paper holder. Hold a level vertical at the mark, and make small pencil marks up the wall. Put a strip of low-tack tape on the wall, its inner edge at the marks. With the level and a yardstick, measure 31 inches across from the first tape; mark the distance and apply a second vertical tape. Hold the level horizontally at the bottom of the fixture (or at a mark indicating a measurement from the floor), make two small marks atop the level *(above)*, and apply the bottom tape just under them.

2 Making the rectangular template. On poster board, use a carpenter's square to lay out a rectangle the full size of one rectangular pane. Working on a cutting board, cut carefully along the lines, using a craft knife and a metal straightedge guide *(above)*.

Next, measure and cut a strip of poster board to be used as a compass *(inset)*. Make the compass ½ inch wide; its length should be twice the width of the rectangle. With a pushpin, punch a hole ½ inch from one end. Measuring from this hole, draw one mark half a pane's width away (here, 5 inches), a second mark ½ inch from the first, and a third mark a full pane's width from the second. At each mark, use the pushpin to make a hole just big enough for the point of a ball-point pen.

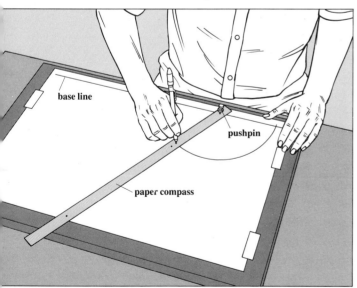

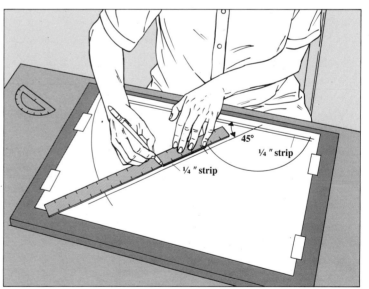

3 Drawing the semicircular template. Onto a wood cutting board, tape a rectangle of poster board measuring 2½ pane widths across and 1½ pane widths high (here, 25 inches by 15). Draw a base line the whole length of the sheet, ½ inch from one long edge. Stick a pushpin through the first hole of the compass and into the base line, at a distance half a pane's width plus ½ inch (here, 5½ inches) from one corner. Put the penpoint into the hole that is 5 inches from the pushpin and swing an arc 180°, creating a semicircle that sits on the base line. Remove the compass.

4 Drawing the top curved pane. Use a protractor and straightedge to draw a line between the pushpin hole and the top of the paper at a 45° angle to the base line. Pin the compass to the paper at the base line, and place the penpoint into each of the other two holes to swing two more arcs outside the first; one will be ½ inch away, the other 10½ inches away. Extend each arc only from the base line to the 45° line.

To complete the semicircular template, make two marks inside the semicircle ¼ inch from the straight side; draw a line through these marks to indicate the bottom of the pane. To complete the curved-pane template *(above)*, similarly mark off a ¼-inch strip from each straight side. ▶

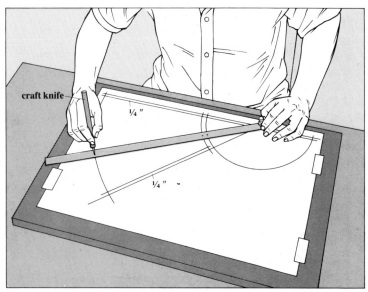

5 **Cutting out the templates.** Pin the poster-board compass in place as before. Insert the tip of a craft knife in the farthest penpoint hole, and swing the knife in an arc, cutting along the outer arc of the curved pane (*above*). Move the knife tip to the next hole and cut along the inner arc of the pane; cut the curve of the semicircle the same way. Finally, use the craft knife with a metal straightedge to cut the straight sides of both templates. Place the mirror face down on a padded worktable. With a felt-tipped marker, draw around the three templates in turn to outline one semicircle, four curved pieces and nine rectangles on the back of the mirror. Tailor one pane to fit around the toilet-paper holder by measuring the fixture and outlining its shape in the corner of one rectangular pane.

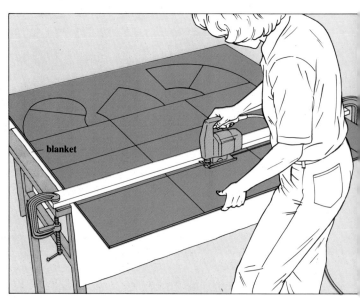

6 **Cutting the mirror.** Position the mirror with the first straight line overhanging the table by half the width of your saber saw's shoe plate. Plac board atop the mirror and exactly over the table edge; secure board and mirror with C clamps. Insert a scroll-sawing blade with 10 teeth to inch into the saber saw and cover the underside of its shoe plate with masking tape. Cut along the overhanging line with the saw. Reposition the mirror and reset the board and C clamps for each cut. Make all of the curved cuts freehand, with a helper steadying the mirror.

9 **Finishing the rows of rectangles.** Have your helper align the two spacers with the boundary tapes at the lower right-hand corner of the design. Distribute pieces of foam tape on another rectangular pane, stand it on the bottom spacer, slide it against the side spacer and firmly press it into place. Next, have your helper hold one spacer under the central space in the bottom row and the other against one corner pane; prepare a rectangular pane, stand it in place in the corner formed by the two spacers and mount it. Mount the second row of panes in the same way, with your helper forming a corner with the two spacers — one spacer atop the first row of panes, the other against the side of a lower pane (*above*). Repeat for the third row.

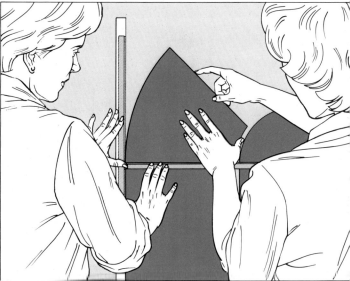

10 **Mounting the semicircle and the outer curved panes.** Have your helper hold the spacer atop the center pane in the third row. Prepare the semicircular pane with tapes equal in total length to twice its straight side, stand it atop the spacer and mount it, centered over the pane below it. Similarly mount the curved panes at each side of the semicircle, standing them atop one spacer and aligning them with the other spacer held in place along the boundary tapes at the sides (*above*).

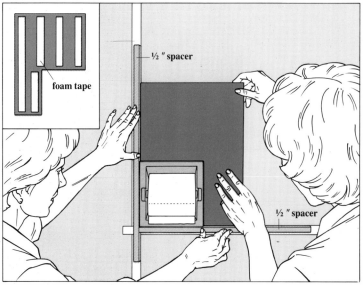

7 **Finishing the edges.** Use a square-cornered, but not sharpened, metal edge — such as the back of a hacksaw blade — to scrape the tool marks off the edges of the cutout mirror pieces. Keep the metal edge at a right angle to the surface of the mirror so as to make flat edges, and scrape always toward yourself for maximum control. Hand sanding with 220-grit sandpaper on a sanding block also works well.

8 **Mounting the first pane.** Start with the pane you have trimmed to go around a fixture (or, if there is none, with a pane for the lower left-hand corner). Cut a strip of 1-inch-wide double-faced foam tape three times the pane's length. Then cut the strip into four or five pieces and distribute them evenly on the pane's back *(inset),* keeping the tapes at least ¼ inch from the edges; peel the protective paper from each tape. Have your helper hold one spacer under the fixture and one beside it, aligned with the boundary tapes. Stand the pane atop the bottom spacer, line it up with the fixture and the side spacer, and press it very firmly into place.

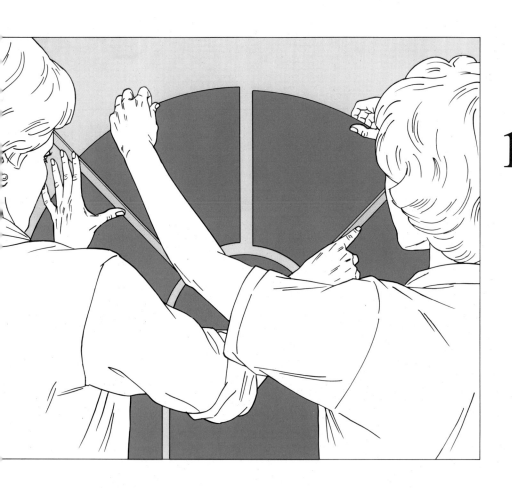

11 **Completing the curved top.** Have your helper hold the spacers against the upper straight sides of the two curved panes you just mounted. Before applying tape to the last two panes, position them in the remaining space, sliding each pane toward the semicircle until their lower curved edges form a smooth curve ½ inch from the semicircle. If the space left between these two panes is more or less than ½ inch, adjust their positions to distribute the space around them equally; mark the adjusted positions on the wall with low-tack tape. Then apply foam tapes and mount the last two panes.

Peel off the protective coverings from all of the panes, beginning at a corner of each pane and pulling downward, not away from the wall. Remove the pieces of boundary tape.

Soft light to frame a mirror

Joined end to end, the fixtures shown below can form continuous ribbons of light to frame almost any size of mirror. Their tubular lamps, or bulbs, with incandescent filaments offer even, glare-free light that is both warm and complimentary. And triangular reflectors that fit onto the sides of the fixtures help diffuse the light. More practically, the reflectors cover the electric boxes over which the fixtures are usu-

ally installed: One reflector will widen the fixture enough to cover a 2-inch box; two, as here, are needed for a 4-inch box.

The fixtures and reflectors are available from lighting-fixture and electric-supply dealers in 12-, 20- and 40-inch lengths and in mat or polished black, gold and silver finishes. Installing these or other incandescent fixtures is a simple matter, as demonstrated at right, when they replace old incandescent lights and utilize

existing electric boxes. Otherwise, yo should have a licensed electrician mov or install the boxes for the fixtures.

Proceed with care on the work you d yourself. First, and above all, turn o the power to the bathroom and adjacer rooms at the service panel, by switchin off the circuit breaker or removing th fuse that serves the rooms. Then mak sure the power is off by using a voltag tester, an inexpensive device consistin of two metal probes and a small bulb tha lights up when the probes are charge with electricity.

Take care never to touch live wire with anything but the voltage-teste probes. Some electric boxes may contai extra wires supplying electricity to ci cuits other than the fixture circuit, so b sure to touch even the probes only t those wires that connect directly to th fixture itself — the others may be liv even after you have turned off the powe Wear rubber-soled shoes, and neve touch any part of the plumbing or stan on a damp floor while at work on wirin When you are done, check your wor with a voltage tester to ensure that th new fixtures are grounded and none of th wires are crossed.

five-part unit. The assembly at right consists of the fixture's base, its cover and a lamp (or bulb), plus two optional side reflectors. The fixture base is wired to the electric box, then the cover is screwed down. The two lengthwise bases of the bulb fit through holes in the cover and snap into clips on the fixture base. When fixtures are linked together, supplementary wires are fed into the bases through holes made by pushing out the knockouts — or removable disks — at the ends of the bases.

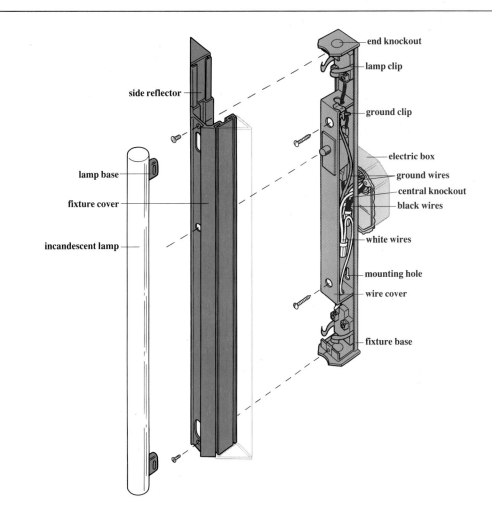

Materials List

Fixtures	4 polished silver fixtures, 12 " long
Reflectors	8 polished silver reflectors, 12 " long
Bulbs	4 35-watt soft-white incandescent bulbs, 12 " long
Wire	36 " length 18-gauge black wire 36 " length 18-gauge white wire 36 " length 18-gauge ground wire, either bare copper or covered with green insulation
Wire caps	10 wire caps for 18-gauge wire
Screws	8 No. 8 round-head screws 8 No. 6 flat-head screws, ¼ " long
Anchors	8 plastic anchors for No. 8 screws

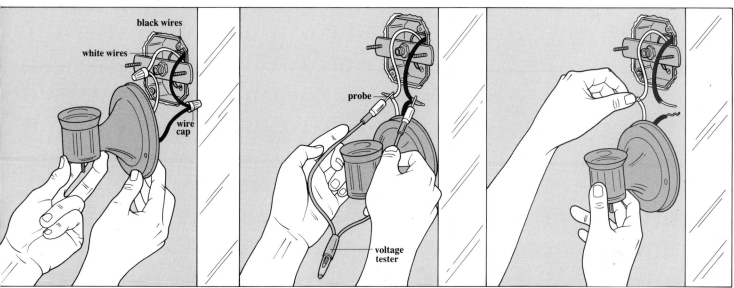

Removing old fixtures. Turn off the power at the service panel. Remove the screws or nuts holding the base of the old fixture in place and gently pull it away from the wall to expose the wires of the electric box *(above, left)*. Carefully remove the wire caps or tape covering the connections between the supply and fixture wires. Restore the power at the service panel and fixture switch, and test to ensure that the box is grounded, taking care not to touch the box itself or any exposed wires: For a metal box, hold one probe of a voltage tester against the box and the other against the bare ends of the black wires; for a plastic box, hold one probe against the black wires and the other against the ground wires. If the box is properly grounded, the tester bulb will

light; if not, call an electrician to have the box grounded. Then turn the power off again. To make sure the power is off, turn the fixture switch to the ON position and hold one probe of the voltage tester against the bare ends of the black wires and the other probe against the grounded electric box; then test from the black wires to the white wires *(above, center)*, and from the white wires to the box. The bulb will not light at any time if the power is indeed off. Separate the wires *(above, right)* and set the disconnected fixture aside. Remove any metal strap or grooved nipple that secured the old fixture. If you are replacing a pair of fixtures, follow the same procedures to remove the other fixture, skipping the test for power if both fixtures are controlled by a single switch. ▶

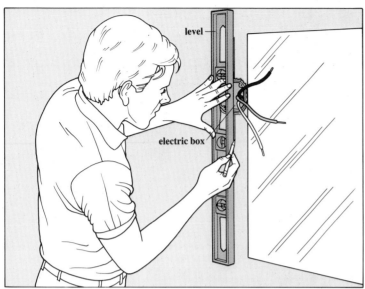

2 **Drawing the locator line.** Use a pencil to mark the wall just above the horizontal midpoint of one electric box. Hold a level plumb against the mark and draw a vertical line that extends about 3 inches above and 18 inches below the mark; the line will be covered by the fixtures.

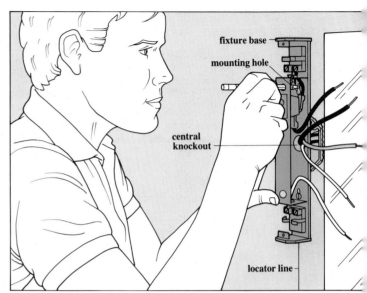

3 **Installing the upper fixture base.** Grasp a base, with the narrow ends of the keyhole-shaped mounting holes upward. Center the base over the electric box, aligning the holes with the locator line. Mark through the holes' narrow ends; set the base down. Drill at the marks using a ¼-inch twist bit and insert plastic anchors for No. 8 screws. Feed the black, white and ground wires from the box through the large knockout in the base's back. Attach the base to the wall with No. 8 screws. Note: If the old fixture had no ground wire, install a 12-inch length in the box. For a metal box, loop one end of the wire around a self-tapping sheet-metal screw fastened tightly to the back of the box; for a plastic box, connect the wire to the other ground wires in the box with a wire cap.

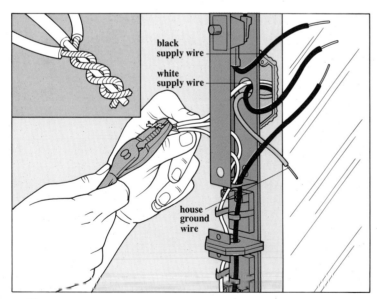

6 **Wiring the fixtures to the electric box.** Join the top end of the white connecting wire and the free end of the white wire built into the upper fixture base. Use slip-joint pliers to wrap the ends clockwise together with — or around — the white supply wire from the electric box. Twist the three black wires together in the same way.

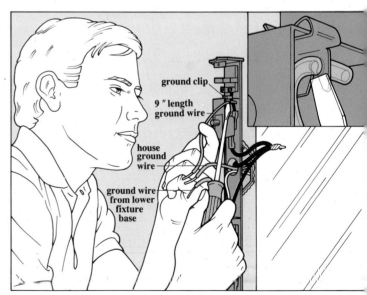

7 **Grounding the fixtures.** Cut two 9-inch lengths of ground wire. Feed one wire through the joined knockouts, routing it through the outside loops of the lamp clips and the oval holes in the ends of the wire covers. Use a screwdriver to wedge the wire's lower end into the ground clip attached to the inside of the wire cover. Wedge one end of the other 9-inch length of ground wire into the ground clip on the upper fixture base (*above and inset*). Strip ½ inch of insulation from the two unattached wire ends, and use slip-joint pliers to twist them clockwise with — or around — the ground wire from the electric box.

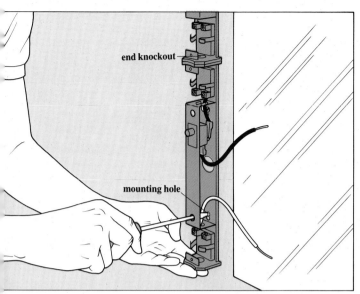

Installing the lower fixture base. Hold another fixture base below the mounted one so that their ends are flush and touching. Mark the locator line through the narrow, top ends of the mounting holes. Put the fixture base down and drill holes at the marks using a ¼-inch twist bit. Push plastic anchors for No. 8 screws into the holes. Use your finger or a screwdriver to remove the round knockouts in the bottom end of the mounted fixture base and the top end of the unmounted one. Mount the lower fixture base with No. 8 screws.

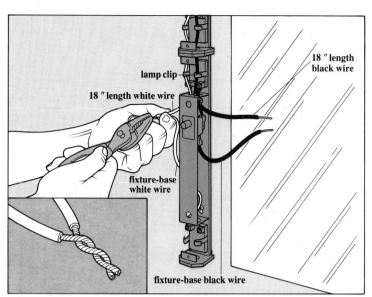

Wiring the fixtures together. Cut 18-inch lengths of black and white wire and use a wire stripper to pull ½ inch of insulation from all four ends. Feed these connecting wires through the joined knockouts, routing the wires through the outside loops of the lamp clips and then through the small oval holes in the ends of the wire covers. Join the lower end of the white connecting wire and the free end of the white wire built into the lower fixture base by twisting them clockwise together with ordinary slip-joint pliers. Join the black wires similarly.

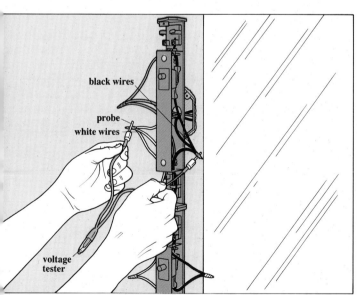

Testing the finished wiring. Repeat Steps 2-7 to mount the second pair of fixtures. Be sure none of the wire connections touch the fixtures or one another. Turn on the power at the service panel and the fixture switch. Touch one probe of the voltage tester to one upper fixture's black wires and the other probe to the white and ground wires in turn; the tester should light in each case. Then check from the white to the ground wires; the tester should not light. If it lights at the wrong time, or fails to light when it should, turn off the power and recheck your wiring. Repeat for the lower fixture's black and white wires, then for the other fixtures. Turn off the power, cap all wire connections with twist-on wire caps and pack all wires neatly under the wire cover.

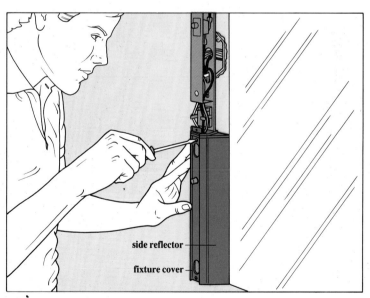

Installing the covers. Slide the triangular reflectors onto the tracks of a fixture cover and fit the cover over a mounted fixture base, making sure the round hole in the cover fits over the white cutoff switch-plunger sticking up from the top of the base. Fasten the top and bottom of the cover to the base with ¼-inch No. 6 flat-head screws. Repeat for the other fixtures, insert the lamps and turn on the power.

Diffused light from above

Depending on your bathroom's style, you may prefer inconspicuous mirror lighting to the bold chrome fixtures shown on the preceding pages. If so, the classic solution is a lighting soffit — a ceiling-mounted wooden box that conceals recessed fluorescent fixtures, which gently bathe your face in a shadow-free glow.

One aspect of the soffit's design depends on the orientation of the ceiling joists in your bathroom. The soffit's two hanging bars are fastened to joists and so must run perpendicular to them — along the sides of the soffit if the joists are parallel to its ends, or vice versa.

To provide adequate light, the soffit should be about 18 inches wide to hold three fluorescent fixtures, or channels, side by side. If the soffit's length does not need to match exactly that of a mirror or vanity, choose the fluorescent channels first and make the soffit just long enough to fit them. If your soffit must be a particular size, with an interior length more than 2 inches longer than standard fixtures, use instead three pairs of shorter fixtures, overlapping their tubes by at least 2 inches (insets, Steps 5 and 6).

The best fixtures for a soffit are single-tube fluorescent channels with rapid-start ballasts. The channels should not have reflectors, a function better served by flat white paint inside the soffit. Use fluorescent tubes labeled warm white deluxe; their light matches the spectral character-istics of incandescent bulbs. The soffit diffuser, a sheet of clear plastic designed to scatter light, can be purchased from electric or plastic suppliers.

The soffit fixtures, of course, will need to be wired to a wall switch. If the soffit supplanting an old switch-controlled fix-ture, the old switch can be left unaltered and wires can be run from the electric box behind the old fixture to the soffit. The drawings at the bottom of the opposite page show the wiring routes from an old fixture mounted on the ceiling (left) or on the wall (right). Alternatively, you can in-stall a new wall switch, drawing power from a nearby switch or receptacle.

Although a knowledgeable amateur can run wires to a soffit, you may prefer to hire a professional electrician. In either case your locality may require an electri-cal construction permit and an inspec-tion. To ensure that the soffit poses no fire hazard, local electric codes generally specify these construction details:

The fixtures must be mounted on a fire-resistant surface, such as plaster or wall-board, rather than on wood. The cable entering a fluorescent fixture must con-tain wires approved for use at tempera-tures of 90° C. (184° F.) — effectively ex-cluding cable made before the mid-1980s. The cable must be physically protected where it passes through the ceiling. And because the ballast generates consider-able heat, wires cannot run beside it.

The simplest way to satisfy these stric-tures is to conceal a large junction box in the ceiling above the fixtures, with new cables running from the junction box to each fixture or to each pair of overlapping fixtures. Where they pass through the ceiling, the cables are protected by short sleeves of thin-wall conduit.

The trickiest part of the electrician's task is getting wires to the new junc-tion box. If the soffit is installed beneath an unfinished attic, holes can be drilled from the attic through the wooden wall framework or the ceiling joists, and the wires can then be threaded, or "fished," through the walls and ceiling. In less con-venient situations, several access holes in the wall or ceiling are needed.

After the soffit is installed, its joints with the walls and ceiling are filled with acrylic caulk. Then the soffit and bath-room are painted together, to conceal any patched wallboard and to ensure that the soffit's hue matches that of the ceiling.

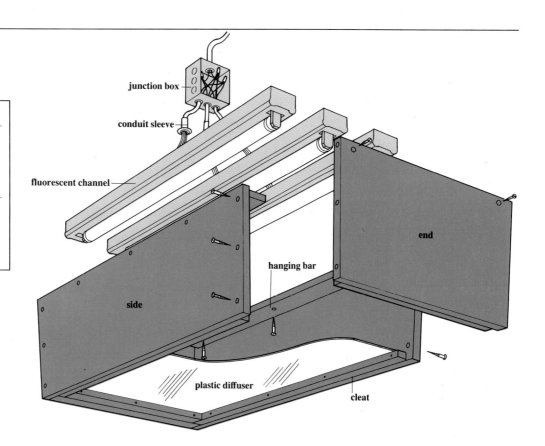

Materials List

Lumber	All pieces cut to match your soffit's dimensions: clear pine 1-by-10 sides and ends 4 cleats of ¾″-square molding stock 2 clear pine 1-by-2 hanging bars
Hardware	about 30 No. 8 flat-head wood screws, 1½″ long about 12 No. 10 round-head wood screws, 2″ long about 30 brads, 1¼″ long about 9 Molly® bolts or toggle bolts

junction box

conduit sleeve

fluorescent channel

end

hanging bar

side

plastic diffuser

cleat

n overhead lighting system. The soffit is ▯box of pine 1-by-10s fastened together with ▯rews and glue. At the box's bottom, ▯eats of square molding support a plastic dif-▯ser. The soffit is suspended from the ▯iling joists by two hanging bars. A junction ▯x mounted above the soffit houses the ▯ectric connections between a single supply ▯ble and the separate cables that run to ▯e fluorescent channels.

How an Electrician Gets Power to a Soffit

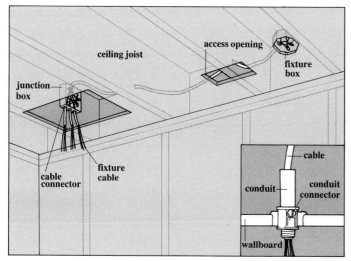

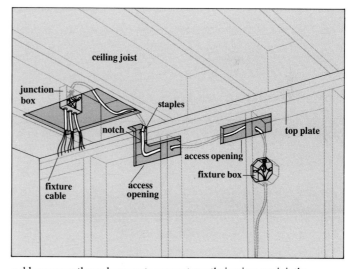

The most time-consuming aspect of wiring a soffit is running concealed cables from one place to another after the soffit's fixture positions are marked on the ceiling *(Step 5)*. To carry power from an old ceiling fixture to a soffit, an electrician can thread, or "fish," the cable between joists if its route runs parallel to the joists. If the cable has to run perpendicular to the ceiling joists *(above, left)*, an electrician must use a wallboard saw to cut a 3-by-6-inch access opening in the ceiling beneath each joist, then drill a ¾-inch hole through the joist for the cable.

Whatever the cable's route, a large opening must be cut above the soffit's planned location so a square 4¹¹⁄₁₆-inch junction box can be mounted on the side of a joist. The electrician turns off the power at the circuit breaker or fuse that controls the old fixture, testing the fixture *(page 61, Step 1)* to make sure that the power is off. A cable connector is installed in a knockout hole of the old fixture box, then the cable is pulled through the connector and its wires are joined to the matching supply wires with wire caps. From the junction box, three short fixture

cables are run through separate connectors; their wires are jointly connected to matching wires from the new supply cable.

To get power to the soffit from a wall fixture *(above, right)* an electrician drills through studs as he would through joists, but atop the wall he encounters two horizontal 2-by-4s called top plates. Here a 4-inch-long access opening is sawed and chiseled in the wall, a matching 2-inch opening is cut in the ceiling, and a ¾-inch-deep notch is chiseled into both top plates. The cable is fastened into the notch with cable staples and covered with a steel plate. The job then proceeds as above.

When the wiring is finished, the fixture box and junction box are covered with steel plates and the ceiling and wall openings are patched with wallboard. Holes for the three new fixture cables then are drilled in the ceiling and the cables are fished through them. The cables are protected by short sleeves of ⅝-inch thin-wall conduit *(inset, above left)*, which are secured in the holes with drywall joint compound.

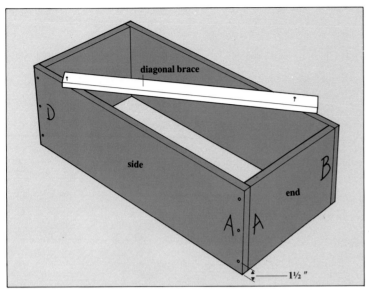

1 Making the box. Fasten a sidepiece and an endpiece together with corner clamps, the end butting the side. Drill three evenly spaced ¹¹⁄₆₄-inch-diameter shank holes through the long board and counterbore them with a ⅜-inch bit. Then drill ⁵⁄₆₄-inch pilot holes through the shank holes into the short board. To forestall later confusion, faintly mark both boards at the joint with the same letter. Drill and mark the other joints the same way. Next, apply a thin bead of glue to the ends of each short board and fasten the soffit snugly together with No. 8 flat-head wood screws 1½ inches long. Flex the soffit until its two cater-cornered measurements are identical, then nail a temporary diagonal brace between the two long boards and tighten all of the screws.

2 Making the lip. Let the glue dry overnight, then remove the diagonal brace. Cut two cleats of ¾-inch-square molding stock to fit along the inside of the soffit's long sides. Spread a thin bead of glue on each piece and place it inside the soffit, flush with the edge of a long 1-by-10. Fasten the molding to the 1-by-10 with 1¼-inch brads every 8 inches (above). Cut two short pieces of molding to fit between the long ones and attach them to the short 1-by-10s in the same way.

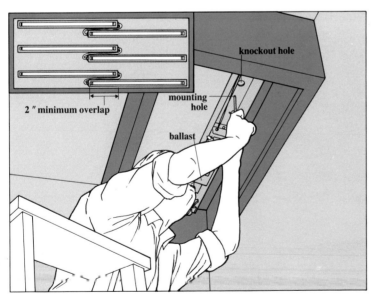

5 Aligning the fixtures. On three identical fixtures use a screwdriver to push inward a metal knockout disk in each fixture's back far from the ballast. Twist the disk free with pliers. Mark the ceiling ½ inch inside the soffit's front and back edges. Hold a fixture against each set of marks in turn, placing the knockout hole near the prospective power source, and trace the locations of the fixture's knockout and mounting holes on the ceiling (above). Center a fixture in the soffit and mark its holes similarly. (If your soffit requires three pairs of fixtures, overlap the ends away from the ballast (inset); mark the positions of the back knockout holes for one fixture in each pair.) Remove the soffit and have an electrician install all the necessary boxes and wiring.

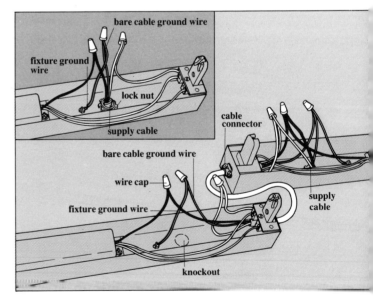

6 Wiring the fixtures. At the service panel, turn off the power to the new cables and test their wires to ensure that the power is off (page 61, Step 1). Replace the soffit and paint its interior surfaces, including the section of ceiling it encloses, with flat white alkyd paint. Fasten the fixtures to the ceiling with Molly bolts or toggle bolts and tighten a lock nut onto each conduit connector. Cut the protruding cables to about 8 inches and strip off their sheathing. Using wire caps, connect each supply wire to the matching fixture wire as shown in the inset. For six fixtures, mount the pairs ½ inch apart, overlapping the ends by at least 2 inches. Remove knockouts from adjacent ends, run a cable between them and join its wires to the fixture and supply wires.

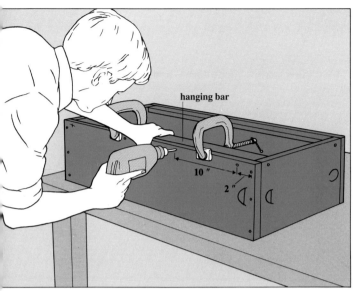

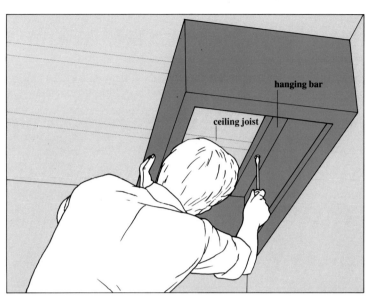

3 Installing hanging bars. For ceiling joists that run parallel to the soffit's long sides, cut two 1-by-2s that match the interior length of its ends; for joists that run perpendicular to the long sides *(above)*, cut two 1-by-2s to fit between the ends. Clamp each hanging bar in place and drill $^{11}/_{64}$-inch shank and $^{3}/_{8}$-inch counterbore holes in the soffit $^{3}/_{8}$ inch from its top edge, placing the holes 2 inches from the bar's ends and at about 10-inch intervals between. Drill additional shank and counterbore holes for screws that will be driven into the ends of each hanging bar. Drill $^{5}/_{64}$-inch pilot holes through the shank holes into the hanging bars, then fasten the bars with glue and No. 8 screws. Sand the soffit with fine (150-grit) paper and fill the counterbores and end grain with spackle.

4 Hanging the soffit. On the ceiling, mark the soffit's planned location and the center of each nearby joist *(page 124, upper right)*. If the joists are perpendicular to the soffit, measure from a side wall to each joist and subtract the distance (if any) between the wall and the soffit's adjacent end. Then measure the resulting dimension from the end of the soffit and mark the hanging bars. If the joists are parallel to the soffit, measure from the back wall to each joist, then mark the hanging bars accordingly. Drill $^{3}/_{16}$-inch shank holes at the marks. Hold the soffit against the ceiling, with a helper if necessary, and mark the ceiling through the shank holes. Remove the soffit and drill $^{3}/_{32}$-inch pilot holes at the marks, then temporarily fasten the soffit *(above)* with No. 10 screws 2 inches long.

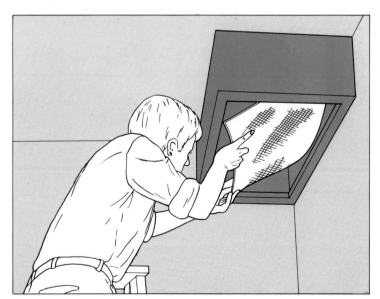

7 Checking the lights and cutting the diffuser. Fold the wires neatly into each fixture and install the fixture covers and fluorescent tubes, then restore the power and test the new lights.

Now measure the length and width of the soffit's interior above the cleats, subtract ½ inch from each dimension and cut a plastic diffuser to this size: Deeply score the diffuser's smooth face with a utility knife and a metal straightedge *(above)*. Then bend the scored line over the edge of a worktable until the plastic snaps.

8 Installing the diffuser. Bend the diffuser's long dimension into a gentle curve and slide a long edge up into the soffit until the entire diffuser clears the soffit's cleats. Then let the diffuser unbend and slide downward until it rests squarely on the four cleats.

The beauty of marble from a paintbrush

Upon first glance, the walls of the powder room below appear to be tiled with marble. But it is not marble at all; the luxurious look was achieved with an inexpensive mixture of oil paints and glaze, applied in bold geometric patterns. Here, there are marbles of green, gray and black. Any one or two could be used alone, or colors such as beige, burnt orange or deep pink could substitute with aplomb.

Creating this grand illusion begins with preparing the walls. Wallpaper should be removed; paint should be washed with a mild solution of household ammonia and water; cracks and holes should be filled with vinyl spackling compound, and any bumps smoothed with medium (100-grit) sandpaper. You can paint over molding, baseboard and switch plates — and around fixtures. A base coat of white semigloss alkyd enamel then should be applied with a roller to achieve a uniform surface. Also enamel a scrap of wood so that you can practice on it before attempting to marbleize the walls.

To achieve the tiled appearance, each wall is marked off into one of the patterns diagramed opposite. Before each area of the pattern is marbleized, the edges are outlined with tape to prevent the paint and glaze from bleeding into adjoining areas. Painter's tape, available in paint and hardware stores, works better than masking tape at preventing seepage. can be peeled off the wall without damaging the finish or leaving a sticky residue and can be applied over a painted surface after only three hours' drying time. masking tape is used, reduce its clinging power by brushing talcum powder along its sticky side. Then let painted surface dry overnight before taping over them.

Diamond and oval patterns appear only on walls unbroken by doors, windows or mirrors. Other walls are marked with the pattern's borders; their central space divided like that of the pattern — minus any diamond or oval — then marbleized the background colors (Steps 11-14).

Here, the walls are 3½ feet and 5 feet wide. For a wall 6 feet wide or more, you might divide the space with vertical borders into three panels, making the center panel one and one half times the width of the side panels. Then either alternate diamond and oval designs in the panels, or place a design in the center panel and treat the side panels as you would wall not receiving a diamond or oval.

You will need artist's oil paints for drawing and coloring, a commercially prepared glaze for background shading and japan drier to speed drying time. Applying them requires brushes of several sizes, a sponge and a cloth, and mineral spirits for cleaning brushes. One ounce of glaze covers about 2 square feet of wall. To determine the amount of glaze needed, measure your walls and divide the square footage by 2. The glaze stays wet for about 30 minutes — enough time for you to complete one area of the pattern.

The close-up photograph opposite can serve as a guide to the size and shape of the veins and to the intensity of the background color. Remember, there is no right or wrong version of fantasy marble. If you dislike a pattern, wipe it away with a cloth dampened in mineral spirits.

Once the marbleized walls are completely dry — about 24 hours — protect them with two coats of clear semigloss polyurethane varnish. Dust the walls well before applying the first coat and wait 2 hours before the second coat. To keep the brush flexible, wrap it in aluminum foil or plastic wrap and store it in the freezer, or suspend the bristles in mineral spirits.

he wall patterns. The diagrams at right tail the pattern elements on the marbleized alls shown opposite; the photograph be-w shows a close-up view of the marbling. or pleasing symmetry, the wall's height divided almost in half: The ratio between e top and bottom sections is about 4 to To accentuate the height of the design, the rizontal borders increase in depth from nches at the top to 4½ inches at the center d 5 inches at the bottom. The vertical rders are 3½ inches wide. Each border is vided into thirds. Above the center bor-rs, each wall is divided into quarters; be-w them, the space is divided vertical-— a narrow wall into halves, a wide wall to thirds. Here, the oval occupies a nar-w wall, the diamond pattern a wider one.

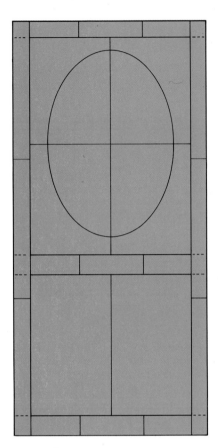

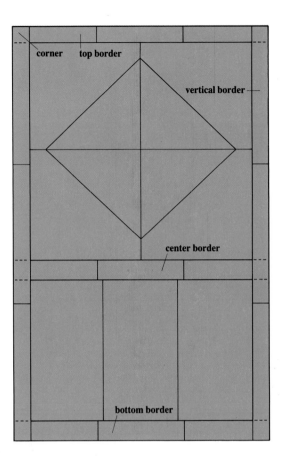

1 **Measuring horizontal borders.** Standing on a stool in a corner of the room, measure down 4 inches from the ceiling with a steel ruler and make pencil marks at the corner and about 6 inches from it. Align a long car-penter's level with the two marks and adjust the level until the bubble is centered. Using the level as a straightedge, draw a line connecting the marks. Then use the level to draw a continuous line across the wall (*above*). At a corner, set the level on the adjacent wall and align the bottom of the level with the drawn line, as shown in the inset. Continue the line across the wall. Repeat these techniques to draw all of the horizontal lines for the borders shown in the diagrams.

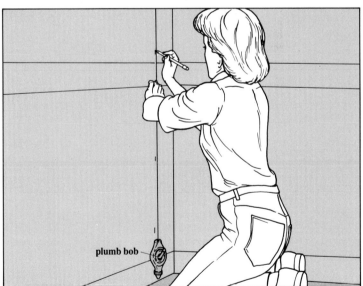

2 **Measuring and marking vertical borders.** Close to the ceiling at a cor-ner of one of the walls, measure in 3½ inches and push a tack into the wall. Pull the string from a plumb bob and hook the tab at the end of the string over the tack. Let the bob fall straight to the floor. Hold the string taut and make pencil marks at about 12-inch intervals from the ceiling to the floor (*above*). Then connect the marks, using the level or a yardstick as a straightedge. Mark each vertical border simi-larly, following the diagrams above. ▶

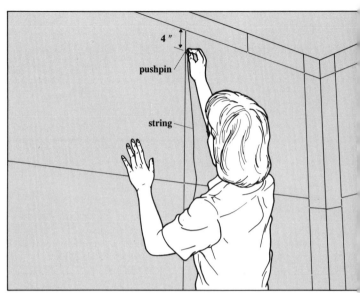

3 **Dividing the bottom wall sections.** Measure the distance between one pair of the vertical borders at a time. On a wide wall, make two sets of pencil marks on the bottom wall section, dividing it into thirds. Using the level, draw a line to connect the marks *(above),* then extend the line to the bottom of the center border and to the top of the bottom border. Similarly divide the narrow walls into two equal sections, and divide each vertical and horizontal border into thirds *(diagram, page 69).*

4 **Dividing the top wall section.** On the wall that is to receive the diamond pattern, make two pencil marks midway between the top and center borders. Connect the marks with a horizontal line, then check the line with a level. Using the same techniques, draw a vertical line midway between the side borders. On the vertical line, make tick marks 4 inches above the center border and 4 inches below the top border. Insert a pushpin through a length of string and into the wall at the top mark *(above).*

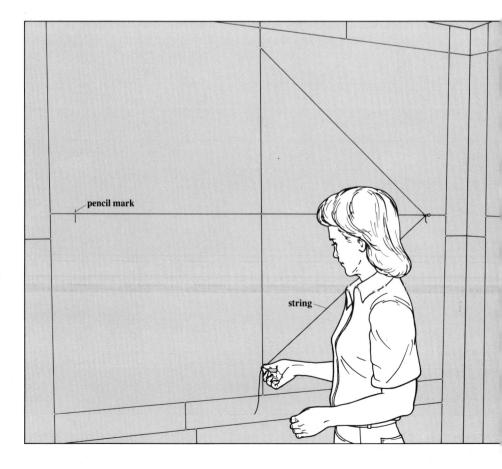

6 **Completing the diamond pattern.** Leaving the side pin in place, move the top pin and string to the pencil mark on the vertical dividing line just above the center border *(right).* Draw a line along the string as before. Now move the side pin and string to the opposite side of the wall, insert the pin at the pencil mark near the side border and draw a line along the string. Then move the bottom pin and string to its original position at the top, and draw the final line along the string to complete the pattern.

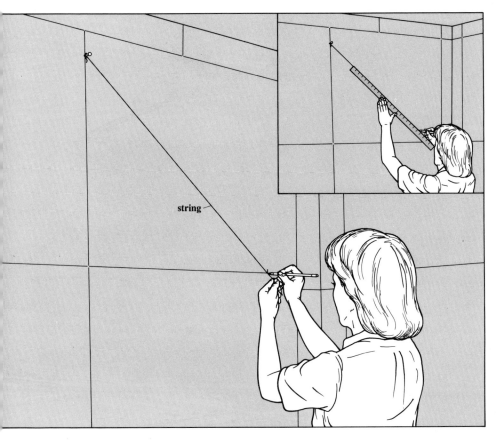

5 **Sizing the diamond pattern.** Stretch the free end of the string down to the horizontal dividing line at the center of the wall. Holding the string taut, adjust its slant until the angle produced by the string and the line is pleasing to your eye. Mark that position on the horizontal line *(left)*. Insert another pushpin through the string and into the wall at that mark. Place a steel ruler alongside the string and draw a line between the pins *(inset)*. Now measure the distance from the side border to the side pin; from the opposite side border measure in this distance on the horizontal line and make a pencil mark.

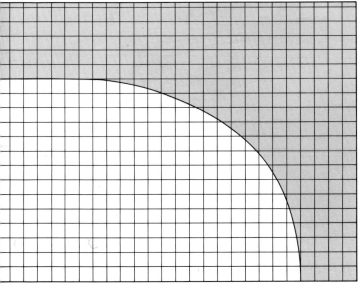

7 **Making an oval template.** Follow the method described in Step 4 to divide the top section of the wall that will receive the oval pattern into quadrants and to make tick marks on the vertical center line. Cut a sheet of poster board or thin cardboard the same size as one quadrant. Rule the sheet off into the same number of squares as in the grid above — 19 vertically and 26 horizontally — and copy the portion of the curving line inside each square in the grid into a matching square on the sheet. Go over the curved outline with your pencil to smooth it before cutting along it with scissors.

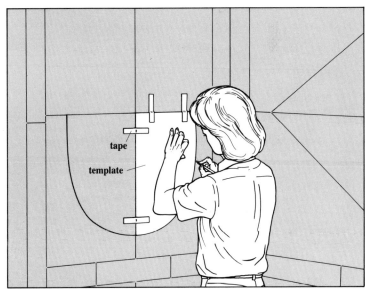

8 **Outlining the oval.** Place the template on the wall, aligning the long straight edge of the template with the vertical center line and the corner of the template's narrow end with the pencil mark on that line. With painter's tape, fasten the template's straight edges to the wall. Then, holding the template flat with one hand, draw around its outside edge with a pencil. Turn the template and retape it as necessary to draw each of the other three curves that complete the oval. ▶

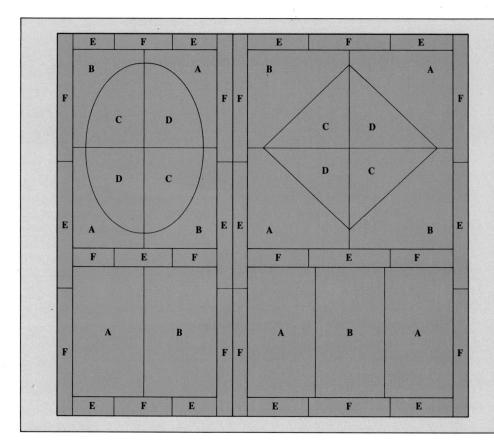

The painting sequence. To create the illusion of marble tiles, marbleize each section of the pattern individually. Begin with the background sections. First paint the sections marked **A** on the diagram at right, let them dry for three hours (or overnight if masking tape is used to shield the painted sections), then proceed to the segments marked **B**. When those areas are dry, paint the pattern sections **C** and then **D** of the oval and diamond designs. Finally, paint the borders, sections **E** and **F**, starting from the top of the walls and ending at the bottom.

10 **Taping pattern sections.** Cut strips of painter's tape slightly longer than the sides of the pattern section you plan to paint first — in this case, section **A** of the background for the diamond. Starting at the end of one side, align the edge of a tape strip with the pencil line, positioning the tape outside the section to be painted; press the tape into place. Repeat for each side of the section, overlapping the ends of the tape at the corners.

Apply tape similarly to all of the other sections designated with the same initial in the diagram above. To tape around curves, cut 1-inch strips of tape and place the side of the first strip on the pencil line. Overlap this strip with the next strip, as close to the line as possible. Add more strips until the area is completely masked *(inset),* then place a cloth over a smooth, hard object such as a spoon and press it along the inside edge of the tape to ensure adhesion around the curve.

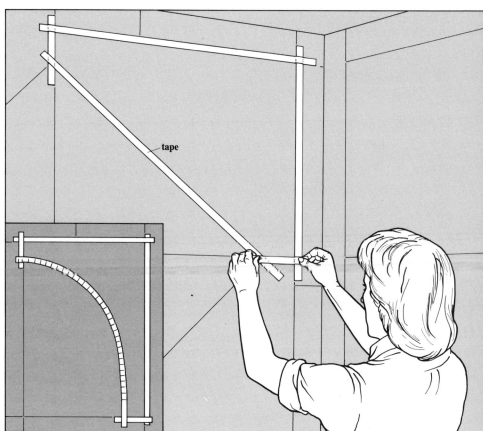

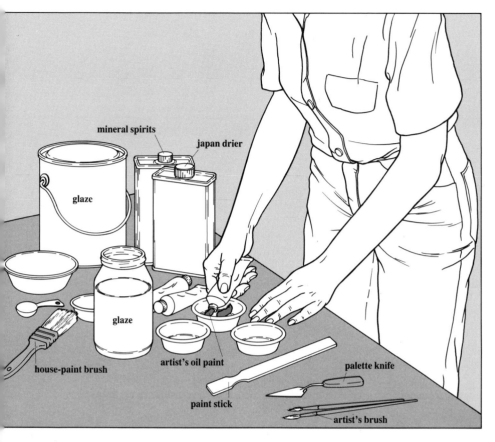

mineral spirits

japan drier

glaze

glaze

house-paint brush

artist's oil paint

paint stick

palette knife

artist's brush

9 **Preparing the paints.** Pour 30 ounces of commercial glaze into a large, widemouthed jar with a lid. Into a small dish squeeze 1 teaspoon (a 1-inch strip) of black artist's oil paint and ½ teaspoon (½ inch) of burnt umber. Transfer 3 tablespoons of glaze from the jar to the dish and mix with a palette knife. Pour the mixture and 1 tablespoon of japan drier into the jar of glaze, and stir with a paint stick. Then pour some of the colored glaze into a clean, shallow bowl.

To prepare the veining colors, squeeze ½ teaspoon each of burnt sienna and burnt umber into another small dish, and mix them together with a palette knife. Squeeze ¼ teaspoon each of burnt sienna and burnt umber into a third dish, but do not mix them. For cleaning the brushes, pour a small amount of mineral spirits into a jar.

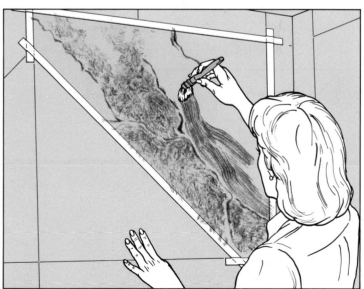

11 **Painting heavy veins.** Holding the handle of a natural-bristle No. 2 artist's brush between your thumb and first two fingers, dip the bristles into the mixed-paint veining color. Beginning on the tape at the edge of the section, press down slightly on the brush's handle to spread the bristles and push the brush along the wall. Vary the width of the vein occasionally by changing the pressure on the brush. Make directional changes in the vein by turning the brush slightly to the right or left every few inches, and add secondary veins that branch off from the first. Paint three or four major veins that flow in the same general direction to suggest the grain of marble.

12 **Glazing the background.** Dip the bristles of a 2-inch synthetic-bristle house-paint brush one third of the way into the colored glaze; tap the brush on the side of the bowl to remove the excess. Then, starting on the tape at the edge of the section, brush the glaze over the open areas: It should just touch, but not cover, the veins. To create different textures, vary the brushstrokes occasionally — for example, use an up-and-down, pouncing motion sometimes, or move the brush quickly back and forth in a scrubbing motion. ▶

13 **Creating light areas.** Tear a small piece off a sponge or crumple a paper towel. Dab the towel or sponge over various areas of the background to lighten the amount of glaze and to give additional texture. Soften any veins that look harsh by dabbing them lightly.

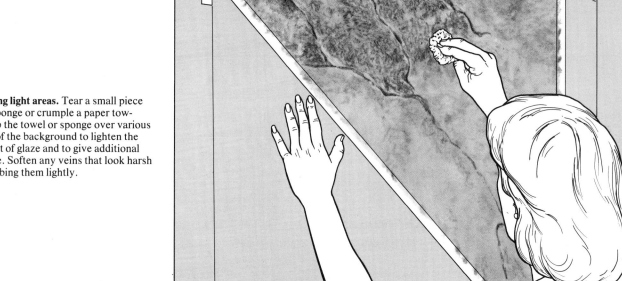

16 **Painting the borders.** Mask the sections of the borders marked **E** on the diagram, page 72. Pour a small amount of white semigloss alkyd enamel into a dish. Open a quart of black semigloss alkyd enamel and stir with a paint stick. Dip the bristles of a 2-inch synthetic-bristle brush one third deep into the black enamel; press the bristles against the rim of the can to remove excess enamel. Apply a light coat to one border section. While the surface is still wet, use a No. 2 artist's brush and the white enamel to paint on heavy veins *(Step 11)* that flow in a generally vertical direction *(right)*. Then change to a No. 1 artist's brush to add a few fine veins *(Step 14)*.

Wait about 30 minutes and peel off the tape; remove any paint that bled into other areas of the border with a cloth dampened in mineral spirits. Now complete the other border sections marked **E** in the diagram. Let the paint dry overnight, then marbleize the remaining border sections, following the sequence in the diagram on page 72.

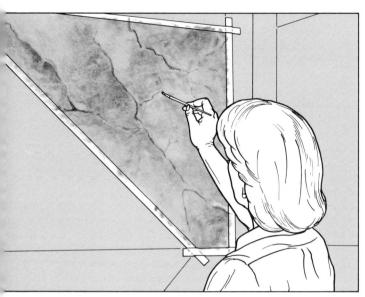

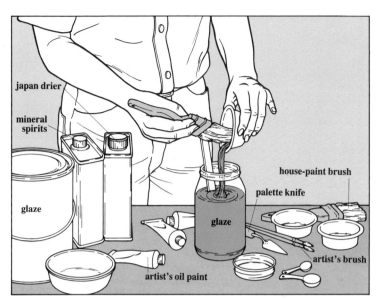

14 **Adding fine veins.** Dip the tip of a natural-bristle No. 1 artist's brush into the burnt umber or burnt sienna. Lightly paint a few fine, spidery lines in the general direction of the heavier veins *(above)*. Vary the paths slightly, and add lines that branch off at shallow angles. Rinse the brush in mineral spirits and wipe it on a rag; change color and paint more fine veins. Wait about 20 minutes, then carefully peel off the tape. If any paint has seeped under the tape, dampen a cloth in mineral spirits to remove it. Now complete the other sections marked **A** in the diagram on page 72. Let the paint dry for three hours (or overnight, if masking tape is used), then tape off the next sections to be painted (marked **B**) and repeat Steps 11-14.

15 **Preparing paints for the diamond and oval.** Pour 22 ounces of glaze into a clean, widemouthed jar with a lid. In a small dish mix together 2 teaspoons (2 inches) thalo green artist's oil paint, 1 teaspoon (1 inch) burnt umber and ½ teaspoon (½ inch) black. Add 3 tablespoons of glaze and stir with a palette knife. Pour the diluted paint and 1 teaspoon of japan drier into the jar of glaze and stir with a paint stick; pour a small amount of the colored glaze into a shallow bowl. Then prepare the veining colors *(Step 9)* and pour a small amount of mineral spirits into a jar. Mask off opposing sections of the diamond and oval designs *(diagram, page 72)*, and use the techniques in Steps 11-14 to marbleize those sections.

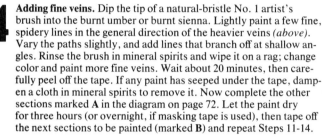

17 **Varnishing the walls.** In a clean, widemouthed jar, dilute 20 ounces of semigloss polyurethane varnish with 4 ounces of mineral spirits; stir with a paint stick. Dip a 3-inch chisel-cut varnish brush halfway into the varnish, and press the bristles against the inside of the jar to remove the excess. At the top corner of a wall, brush on a thin coat in a 1-by-2-foot area, using quick horizontal strokes. Then — without rewetting the brush — start at one side and slightly below the varnished section to make arcing strokes, each placed just inside the previous one, to the top of the section and down again *(left)*, thus smoothing the area. Complete the wall, ending with horizontal strokes across the dry area at the bottom.

Wait 24 hours, then apply a second coat of varnish. Let dry, then rub the walls lightly with 4/0 steel wool and dust them with a cloth.

The luxury of bathroom carpet

Soft, warm carpet is an affordable luxury for any bathroom. Two types are suitable. When wear and tear will be minimal, any conventional carpet made of synthetic fibers — even one with a stiff jute backing — serves well, particularly if you buy sale-priced remnants of fine carpets.

For carpets that will need frequent washing, the best choice is so-called bath carpet, which has a synthetic pile and a pliable latex backing. Small bath carpets can be laundered at home in a regular washing machine using mild soap and warm water, then tumbled dry at low temperature. Large ones should be washed by a commercial laundry.

Both conventional and bath carpets are installed directly over the bathroom floor without carpet padding, which would retain moisture. The carpet is cut to fit the room approximately, then trimmed on the bathroom floor with a sharp carpet knife and a cutting surface such as a large breadboard or a 3-foot piece of plywood or 1-by-12. The knife, along with a packet of replacement blades, a yardstick or a long metal ruler, and a roll of double-faced carpet tape, is available from stores specializing in carpet-laying supplies.

The 2-inch-wide tape that secures the carpet is a convenient but somewhat fragile fastening. To prevent the carpet from bunching up in a large or heavily trafficked bathroom you may need to supplement the usual perimeter tape with diagonal strips every foot or so across the entire floor. Generally you should replace the tape whenever you wash the carpet.

Before buying carpeting, measure the room's length and width and, if possible, get carpet at least 6 inches larger in each dimension. Conventional carpet comes in 12-foot-wide rolls; bath carpet comes in room sizes, such as 5 by 8 feet, and in rolls 6 or 8 feet wide. If one piece will not perfectly fit your bathroom, you will need to patch together two or three sections.

Lay the carpet so that the pile leans toward the bathroom's main entrance, presenting a full, rich appearance. This typically means using the end of a carpet roll across the entrance; check the pile direction by stroking the carpet in whatever direction raises the fibers. When you "look into" the pile, with fibers leaning toward you, the carpet exhibits its deepest hue; from the opposite direction you are "looking over" the pile and the carpet appears flatter and lighter in color.

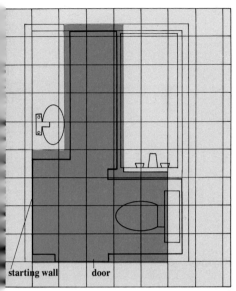

1 **Drawing a diagram.** Measure your bathroom floor and make a scale drawing on graph paper. Plan to start the installation on a side wall adjacent to the longest uninterrupted wall — here, the longest wall includes the doorway. Add a 3- to 4-inch trimming allowance to the diagram along all of the carpet's edges except the one abutting the starting wall. Cut out the diagram, turn it over and mark on its back the starting wall and the position of each piece of carpet.

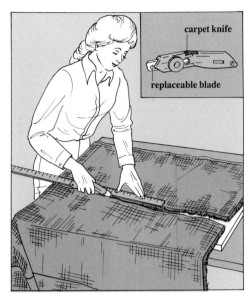

2 **Cutting the carpet.** Put the carpet, backing side up, on the floor or worktable. Using a carpet knife *(inset)* and a cutting board, trim off the selvages — the carpet's tightly woven edges. Starting at a corner where a selvage met the leading edge of the carpet pile, use a yardstick and felt-tipped marker to transfer the diagram in full scale onto the backing. With the yardstick as a guide, cut along the lines *(above)*; change the blade when the knife begins to drag.

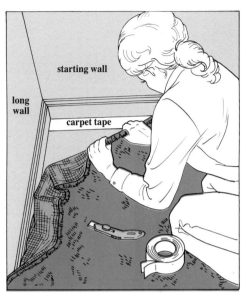

3 **Fitting the first corner.** Set the cut end of a roll of double-faced carpet tape — sticky side down — in the corner where the starting wall and the long wall meet. Unroll the tape, aligning its edge with the starting wall; press it down. Cut the tape at the end of the wall. Position the carpet in the bathroom, smoothing it flat. Pull off the installed tape's paper covering; press the carpet's trimmed edge down against the tape *(above)*.

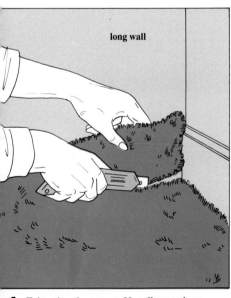

4 **Trimming the carpet.** Unroll tape along the long wall, here the doorway wall, putting separate double strips along the threshold. Smooth the carpet toward the long wall, letting the edge extend upward 3 or 4 inches. Press the carpet onto the tape and trim along the line between the floor and the wall with the carpet knife *(above)*. Cut off narrow strips of excess carpet when it gets in your way. At the doorway, trim the carpet to fit against the threshold.

5 **Fitting around obstacles.** At the toilet or other obstacles, smooth the carpet up to the obstacle and fold back the remainder. Slide a board into the fold, then cut a mirror image of the obstacle's front edge in the top layer of folded carpet. Slash the top layer from the center of the obstacle straight back to the carpet's edge *(above, top)*, creating two flaps. Lay the flaps around the sides of the obstacle *(above, bottom)*; trim them accurately and tape them down.

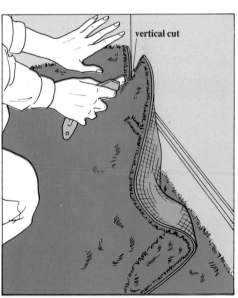

6 **Completing the installation.** Work around the perimeter of the room, taping and trimming each edge as you go. Just before you reach each corner, press the carpet against the wall and make a vertical cut above the corner *(above)*. To fill areas not covered by the main piece of carpet, cut scraps to the size of each uncarpeted section — making sure that the scrap's pile will match that of the main piece. Tape down each added section individually.

A protective sheathing of gleaming tile

Smooth as glass — and as easy to clean — ceramic tiles are an ideal surface for bathroom walls and floors. The tiles come in a range of [co]lors, patterns, sizes and shapes to fit [ev]ery decorating dream. Many are sold [in]dividually; others are already grouped [in] sheets of paper or mesh *(page 86)*. Thin highly glazed tiles usually go on [w]alls, thick mat-finished tiles on floors. [Fl]oor tiles can be used on walls, and both [ty]pes are equally simple to install wher[ev]er the surface is firm, clean and level.

Mark well that walls and floors will be [sl]ightly thickened by the tile. Fixtures [an]d hardware may need to be reseated, [an]d the bathroom door may not clear the [til]es: Remove the door from its hinges [an]d use a crosscut handsaw or a saber [sa]w to trim the bottom by the thickness of [th]e tiles. If your present walls are tiled [pa]rtway, you can use wallboard to level [th]e walls for new tiling *(pages 84-85)*.

To estimate how much tile to buy, cal[cu]late the square footage of each wall and [th]e floor by multiplying height or length [by] width. Add 5 per cent to allow for [w]aste — and replacements in the future.

Have a plumber remove the washba[si]n, toilet, and all bathtub hardware and [di]sconnect water lines. Reattach loose [til]es; drive in any protruding nails. Use a [pr]y bar to remove baseboard or ceiling [m]olding, pulling it away in sections.

Clean the walls by stripping off wall[pa]per or scrubbing paint with a heavy-[du]ty detergent. Sand old tiles and glossy [pa]int so adhesives will stick to them. Us[in]g a putty knife, pack cracks or holes [w]ith vinyl spackling compound. Finally,

turn off the electricity to the room at the service panel and take out all of the electric fixtures and switch and outlet plates.

Installing the tiles is done in four stages: Draw guidelines to form a geometrical layout that makes maximum use of whole tiles *(below)*. Attach tiles to the walls with Type I mastic — an organic adhesive — and to the floor with impact-resistant, cement-based epoxy mortar. Fill the joints between the tiles with a cement-based grout. Finally, caulk the seams where the tiles meet the bathtub.

When both the walls and the floor are to be tiled, the layout starts on a prominent wall — here, the wall behind the bathtub — and continues from one adjacent wall to the next, then to the floor. This way, when a section ends with a partial tile, the rest of that tile usually can be used on the adjacent wall or floor.

Grout joints of 1/8 to 1/4 inch are integral to a tile layout; they let tiles move individually and thereby resist breakage. Many tiles have small projections, called lugs,

on all four edges to ensure even spacing. For plain-edged tiles, cross-shaped plastic spacers fit at the corners. Lugs or spacers are covered up by the grout.

Various adhesives are compatible with different tiles and underlying wall and floor surfaces. For most walls, Type I mastic is the best adhesive. Wet mastic is water-soluble and can be wiped up easily. The adhesive cures in 24 hours to form a water-resistant bond. Thin-set epoxy mortar is usually favored for floors because of its strength and resistance to impact. Grout additives can make grout stain- and mildew-resistant, and there are colors to match or contrast with the tiles.

Tiling tools include a notched metal trowel for spreading adhesives and a rubber-faced float — a sort of wood trowel — for "floating," or applying, grout. A tile cutter for straight cuts and tile nippers for curves can be rented at the tile store. And get safety goggles to shield your eyes when cutting tiles, plus rubber gloves to protect your hands from adhesives.

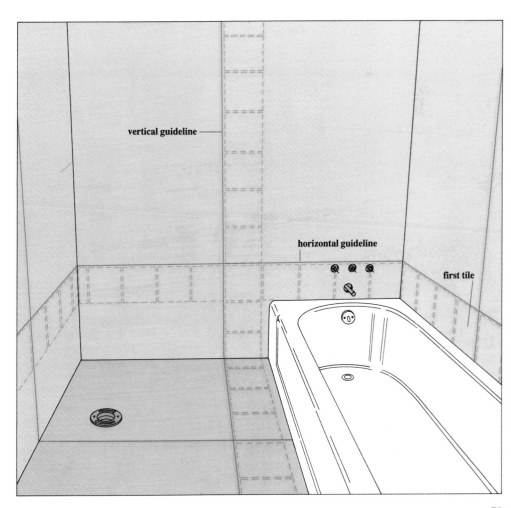

master layout. Intersecting horizontal [an]d vertical guidelines *(solid lines)* drawn on [th]e walls form a basic grid for laying the [ti]le — here, 8-inch-square tiles *(dotted lines)* [se]parated by 1/8-inch grout joints. The [v]ertical lines from the front wall, which faces [th]e door, and from the side wall opposite [th]e bathtub continue the grid onto the floor. [F]or symmetry, partial tile is linked with [p]artial tile, whole tile with whole tile. The [fi]rst tile is laid flush with the tub rim at [th]e intersection of the guidelines on the side [w]all behind the tub. Parallel rows are ex[te]nded halfway up the wall first on one side [o]f the guideline, then on the other. After [th]e other walls are successively tiled halfway [u]p, the tile is extended to the ceiling. Fi[n]ally, the floor is completed.

vertical guideline

horizontal guideline

first tile

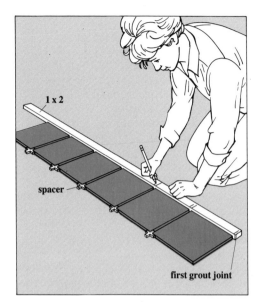

1 **Making a layout stick.** Place a row of tiles — here, 8-inch squares — on the floor alongside a 1-by-2. Draw a line across one end of the board at a distance equal to a grout joint. Set the first tile's outside edge on the line. Place spacers between smooth-edged tiles to represent the grout joints; tiles with lugs should be butted tightly together. Mark each grout joint's width on the board *(above)*. Draw a line to represent the last joint; cut the board at the line.

2 **Establishing the horizontal guideline.** Set a carpenter's level on the rim of the tub — first at the side, then at the head — to check whether the tub is level in both dimensions. If it is, place a tile on the side rim flush against the wall. Make tick marks above each corner of the tile at a distance equal to the width of the grout joints *(above)*. Use the level as a straightedge to connect the marks and to extend this line completely around the room.

If one dimension of the bathtub is not level, set the tile at the lowest end of that rim before drawing the line. If both dimensions slant, set the tile on either rim at the lowest corner.

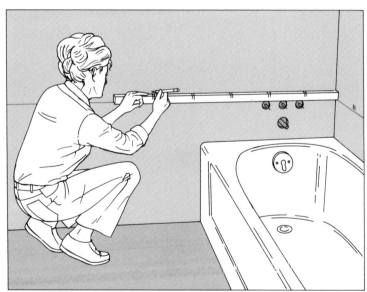

5 **Establishing the vertical guideline beside the tub.** Hold the layout stick on the horizontal guideline above the head of the tub. If the row of tiles behind the tub will finish with a full tile at this corner, push the end of the stick against the side wall. If there will be a partial tile at this end of the row behind the tub, subtract its width from that of a full tile; measure this distance from the corner, mark the horizontal guideline and position the end of the layout stick at the mark. In either case, make tick marks above the guideline wherever the edges of the grout joints will cross it — from the corner end of the layout stick to one full tile width beyond the outer edge of the tub *(above)*.

6 **Marking the remaining vertical guidelines.** Use the chalk line/plumb bob to snap a vertical guideline at the tick mark for the first full tile beside the tub *(above)*. Then, starting at the chalked line and working along the horizontal guideline away from the tub, use the layout stick to determine whether the tiles along this wall will end with a whole or partial tile. Mark the grout joints as you go. Proceed to the adjacent wall, beginning at the corner with a whole or partial tile — according to the last tile on the previous wall. At the center of the wall, snap another vertical guideline. Repeat this procedure of measuring walls with the layout stick and snapping chalked lines all around the room. Then extend the vertical chalked lines to continue the grid on the floor.

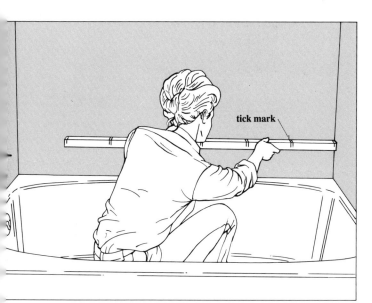

3 **Planning the first tile row.** Place the layout stick on the horizontal line above the tub, with one end of the stick at the corner where the head of the tub meets the side. Draw a tick mark on the line at the opposite end of the stick. Slide the stick along the line to the end of the tub. If the tick mark meets a line on the stick indicating the right-hand side of a grout joint, a row of whole tiles will fit along the wall. If the marks do not align and the space left over is more than 2 inches wide, plan to cut a tile to fit the space when you install the row. If the space left over is less than 2 inches, add it to the width of a tile, divide by 2 and use tiles cut to this width at both ends of the row, with whole tiles between them.

4 **Drawing the first vertical guideline.** Using the layout stick and your calculations *(Step 3)*, make tick marks on the horizontal line where the edges of the grout joints will cross it. Standing on the tub's rim, hold the tab end of a chalk line/plumb bob at the ceiling directly above the grout-line mark nearest the center of the horizontal line. Drive a nail into the wall to hold the tab in place. Step down, unwinding enough of the chalky string so that the plumb bob just reaches the rim of the tub. Flick the string to disperse excess chalk, and allow the bob to hang straight. Pull the chalk line taut, press the bob against the wall and snap the string, making a chalked line on the wall.

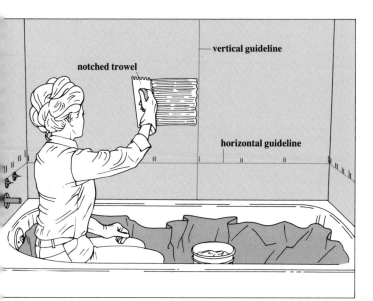

7 **Spreading mastic.** Line the tub with newspaper, brown wrapping paper or cardboard to protect it from nicks from dropping tiles or the trowel. Wearing rubber gloves to protect your hands, load a notched trowel with about a cup of mastic. Beginning on the side wall, spread the mastic over an area of about 4 square feet from the vertical line to the corner; work up to the guidelines, but do not obscure them. Holding the trowel at a 45° angle, with the notched edge against the wall, apply the mastic in a sweeping motion. Press the trowel down and force the mastic through its teeth to distribute the mastic evenly. Wipe up excess.

8 **Laying the tiles.** Set the first tile on the tub rim in a corner formed by the intersecting guidelines. Twist the tile slightly to embed it in the mastic, but avoid sliding the tile and thereby clogging the grout space. If your tiles are smooth-edged, place a spacer at each corner of the installed tile *(inset)* and butt the next tile along the rim against the spacer. If your tiles have lugs on the edges, press the lugs together. After completing one horizontal row, begin another row above it at the vertical guideline; this avoids misaligning the tiles if the wall is out of plumb. Set the tiles to a height of 2 or 3 feet on one side of the guideline, checking their alignment occasionally with the level. With a damp sponge, wipe off any excess mastic that squeezes onto the tile surface. ▶

9 **Anchoring the tiles in the adhesive.** Spread adhesive on the other side of the guideline above the tub and follow the method described in Step 8 to lay tiles there. After completing every few rows of tile, wipe off excess adhesive with a clean, damp sponge. Tap the face of each tile with a rubber-faced float to seat the tiles deeply in the adhesive and level the surface so that no corner sticks up higher than any other. Set no more than half a wall at a time before moving on to the next wall. Once the lower halves of all the walls have been tiled, go back and tile the upper halves straight to the ceiling.

10 **Marking a straight cut.** To produce a narrow tile for the end of a row, align a full-width tile against the previously installed one and slide it over the empty space in the row. Use a felt-tipped pen to mark where the unattached tile's top and bottom edges intersect the end of the installed tile. Then place the marked tile on a flat surface and measure the width of a grout joint from each mark to position marks for cutting the tile.

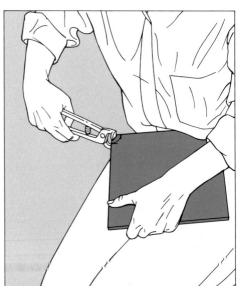

12 **Marking a curved cut.** At circular obstructions, fit a tile against the side of the installed one. Slide it down under the obstruction; use a felt-tipped pen to mark the obstruction's edge on the tile's top edge. Next, align the bottom of the tile with the rim of the tub, as shown. Hold the tile close enough to the obstruction to mark its depth on the tile's side edge. Draw a freehand curve to connect the two marks.

13 **Cutting tile with tile nippers.** Put on safety goggles. Holding the tile firmly, set the jaws of tile nippers about 1/8 inch inside the outlined edge. Squeeze the handles to bite off a small chip of tile. Continue nibbling off small chips until you have reached the cutting line. Test the opening for fit as you go, but do not try to smooth the ragged edges; the escutcheon behind the faucet will later hide them. Install the tile.

14 **Complex fittings.** Where several obstructions block a tile, it has to be halved and each half shaped separately: Mark the tile where the pipe's center meets it (*above*). Cut the tile in half at the mark. Hold each cut section in position on opposite sides of the pipe and mark the width of the pipe on each cut edge. Cut the opening with nippers. Mark and cut the corners at the top outside edge for the faucet stems.

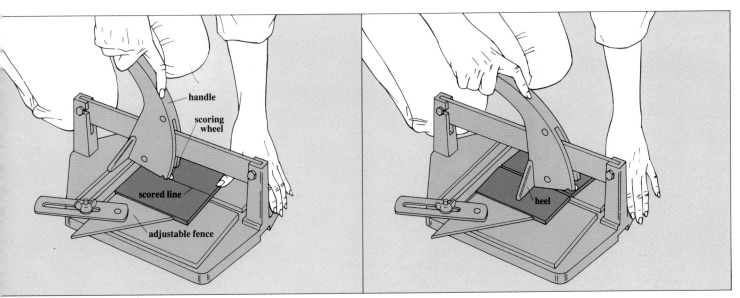

handle

scoring wheel

scored line

adjustable fence

heel

11 **Slicing the tile.** Put on safety goggles to protect your eyes from flying chips or dust. Set the tile on the pad of a tile cutter. Align the cutting marks on the tile with the scoring wheel on the handle. Fasten the adjustable fence against the edge of the tile. Push the handle forward and roll the scoring wheel across the tile by pressing down firmly on the handle and pulling it toward you *(above, left)*. Then lower the handle's heel so that its base is in the center of the tile. Force the handle down sharply to snap the tile along the scored line *(above, right)*. Install the narrow tile.

mortar

spacer

guideline

15 **Setting floor tile.** Mix the mortar, following the manufacturer's directions. With the notched trowel, spread it over the far corner of the floor opposite the tub. Lay the first tile at the corner formed by the guidelines *(above)*, twisting it slightly as you press it firmly into the mortar. Make sure the tile is aligned with the guidelines. Place spacers at the tile's corners and set the first row, cutting tiles to fit as necessary. Set the next row along the other guideline. Then tile the area in between. Check tile alignment repeatedly with a carpenter's square. When you finish the section, tap each tile with the rubber-faced float to create a flat surface. Fill in the corner next to the tub, then continue laying tile to the doorsill.

16 **Cutting slivers of tile.** To cut the thin strips of tile often necessary along a doorsill, first find a narrow scrap piece. Mark it to size and score it with the tile cutter *(Step 11)*, but do not cut it: The tile cutter will splinter a strip of tile less than 2 inches wide. Instead, use the nippers to bite off ⅛-inch chips up to the scored line. If you have no partial tile to work with, cut a whole tile in half, score it to the desired width, then cut it to size with the nippers. ▶

17 **Grouting the walls.** Let the adhesive and mortar cure for 24 hours. Then mix a cement-based grout in a plastic box or bucket, according to the manufacturer's directions. Do not use too much water: Grout that is too wet will not form a solid joint. Work in an area of about 4 square feet at a time. Wearing rubber gloves, trowel the grout into the crevices with a rubber-faced float, holding the float at a 45° angle and decreasing the angle steadily to force the grout completely into the joints. Do not worry about smearing the tile; excess grout wipes off easily with a wet sponge.

Making a Level Surface with Wallboard

In many bathrooms, tile covers only the "tub surround" — the area adjoining the tub — and the tiled area is not on the same plane as the rest of the wall. Before tiling the entire room, you must create a uniformly level surface by building up the untiled portions of the walls with wallboard.

For a standard 5-by-7-foot bathroom, you will need twin sheets of 4-by-8-foot water-resistant wallboard. The thickness of the wallboard should equal the amount that the old tile extends beyond the untiled walls — here, ½ inch. After cutting the wallboard to size and nailing it in place as demonstrated at right, fill in the seams between the wallboard and the old tile with premixed joint compound. Then set the new tile following the steps beginning on page 80.

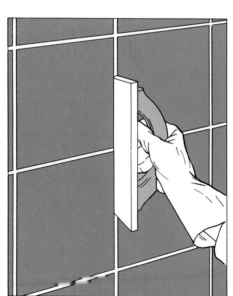

18 **Reinforcing joints.** When all joints in a section are filled, push the float's edge into each joint to tamp the grout. Wipe off excess by drawing the edge diagonally across the grout lines. Wait 20 minutes, then clean the tiles with a wet natural sponge, rinsing it often. Grout the remaining joints. Let the grout dry for two hours; wipe off any film with a soft cloth. Do not walk on the floor or touch the walls for 24 hours.

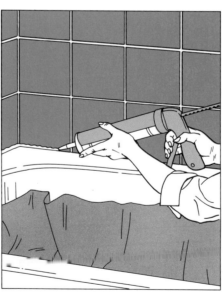

19 **Caulking the tub.** Fit a tube of silicone caulk into a caulking gun and cut off the tip of the tube about ⅛ inch from the edge at a 45° angle. Push the tube tip into one of the gaps between the tile and the tub and simultaneously squeeze the tube while drawing the gun along the gap. Repeat this process to caulk all around the tub.

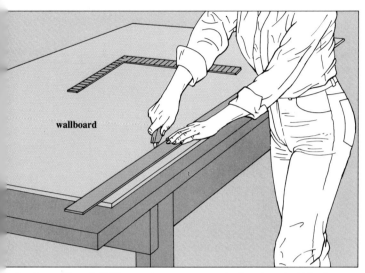

Scoring wallboard. With a steel tape, measure the length and width of each rectangular section of wall not covered by the tile. Plot the arrangement of the rectangles on graph-paper representations of 4-by-8-foot wallboard so that you can cut all of them out of the fewest possible wallboard sheets. Place a sheet of wallboard on a worktable. Using a straightedge and a carpenter's square to make perfect right angles and straight lines, draw the largest rectangle required. Then set the straightedge on a marked line and run a utility knife along it to score the paper surface of the wallboard *(above)*.

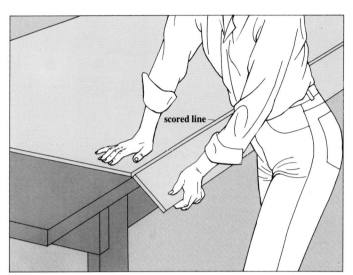

2 **Breaking off scored wallboard.** Slide the wallboard to the edge of the worktable and set the scored line on the table edge, letting the excess board overhang the edge. With one hand holding the board on the table, snap the unsupported section downward all along the scored line to break the gypsum core of the wallboard. With the broken section hanging over the table edge, cut through the paper backing on the underside with the utility knife, following the broken line for about a foot. Then snap the section upward to break off all of the overhanging board. Follow the same procedure to size as many pieces of wallboard as you need.

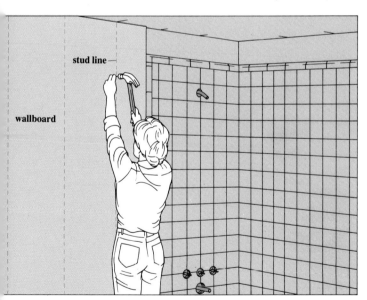

Attaching the wallboard. Locate the studs behind the wall *(page 124)* and mark their positions with pencil on the ceiling and floor. Lift the wallboard into position. Then drive 2-inch-long drywall nails or screws along the stud lines at 18-inch intervals. Butt the next wallboard section tightly against the first and nail the new section to the studs *(above)*.

If you cannot locate studs, fasten the wallboard with wallboard adhesive. To do this, first spread an even coating of wallboard adhesive on a section of wallboard with a notched trowel. Position the wallboard and press it to the wall. While the adhesive is still wet, tap the surface of the wallboard with a rubber-faced float to create a solid glue bond.

4 **Filling the joints.** Scoop up a small amount of premixed joint compound with a wide putty knife. Starting at one end of a tile row, draw the putty knife over the cavity between the wallboard and tile; press hard to force the compound in. Reload the putty knife as often as necessary to fill the cavity along that row; repeat the process wherever tile and wallboard meet. Then fill in any other seams or cracks in the wallboard. Let the compound dry for 24 hours. Use medium (100-grit) paper to sand any rough areas flat enough to allow a tile to lie flush over them.

Tile Sheets: A Timesaver for Floors

Preassembled tiles on 1-foot-square sheets of perforated paper or plastic or fiber-mesh backing can save considerable frustration and time, especially if the tiles are small or irregularly shaped. Sheets are installed much like individual tiles: Guidelines are drawn, sheets — backing and all — are laid in adhesive, then joints between tiles are grouted.

However, when tiling only the floor, as demonstrated here, guidelines and work begin from the corner of the room closest to square — ideally, one on the most prominent wall. This method makes it possible to use the greatest number of whole tiles around the edges and keep tile cutting to the minimum.

Besides calculating the square footage of tiles for the room, measure around the walls to determine the running feet needed for trim tiles along the base of the walls. In this case, the trim pieces are cut from the sheets. Instead, you can use so-called bullnose tiles, with curved top edges.

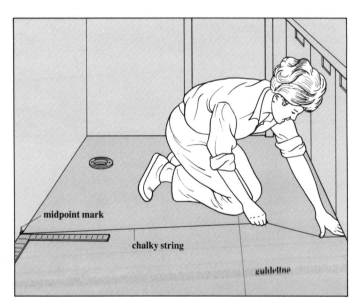

3 **Snapping guidelines.** Set the angle of a carpenter's square at a midpoint mark, with the short leg flush against the wall and the long leg extending into the room. Fasten a chalk line at the midpoint mark with a tack. Stretch the chalky string along the square and across the room to the opposite wall. Lift the string and snap it to leave a guideline on the floor. Repeat between the other two walls. Place the square at the intersection of the guidelines to make sure they meet at right angles. If not, snap them again. Starting at the guideline intersection, spread mortar over a 4-square-foot area *(page 83, Step 15)* in the corner where you will set the first tile sheet.

4 **Setting the tile.** Leaving the backing intact, gently set a tile sheet at the intersection of the guidelines *(above)*, unrolling the sheet slowly and pressing the tiles into the adhesive as you go. Continue setting sheets along the guidelines up to the walls, leaving grout spaces between sheets. To fit around obstructions — here, a toilet flange — turn a sheet upside down and use a utility knife to cut the tiles apart. With a felt-tipped pen, mark the tiles to fit around the obstruction. Then cut them with tile nippers *(page 82, Step 13)* and set them in place. Complete laying the tiles across the floor, working in 4-square-foot sections and making cuts at the end of rows *(page 83, Step 11)* where necessary.

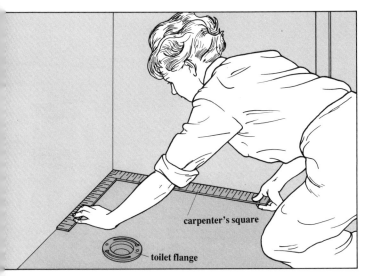

carpenter's square

toilet flange

Finding the corner closest to square. Have the toilet removed. Clean and smooth the floor, and take off any baseboard *(page 40)*. Then place a carpenter's square in a corner where the most prominent wall — usually the wall opposite the door — meets an adjacent wall. If the square fits flush against the walls, plan to begin tiling in that area of the room. If the carpenter's square does not fit flush, move it to the other corners in turn to find one that is square, or nearly so.

midpoint mark

2 **Laying a dry course of tiles.** Starting from the square corner, lay a row of tile sheets along one wall to its midpoint. Leave a grout space between each sheet equal in width to the grout spaces between individual tiles in the sheet. Starting from the corner again, lay another row of tile sheets along the adjacent wall up to that wall's midpoint. Mark the midpoint of each wall with a vertical line near the floor *(above)*. Then pick up the tile sheets.

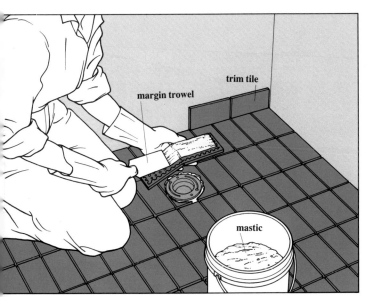

margin trowel

trim tile

mastic

5 **Setting trim.** To cover the base of the walls where they adjoin the floor, use a utility knife to slice off a row of tiles — here, a row of two — from a sheet of tile. Holding the row of trim tile in one hand, spread Type I mastic on the back of each tile with a margin trowel *(above)* or one side of a regular trowel. Press the tiles against the wall at a corner, leaving only the space of a grout joint and butting the lower edges tightly against the floor tile. Add the next row of trim alongside the first, leaving a grout space between the two. At the opposite corner of the wall, mark and cut individual tiles as necessary to get a perfect fit. Allow the tile 24 hours to set before grouting.

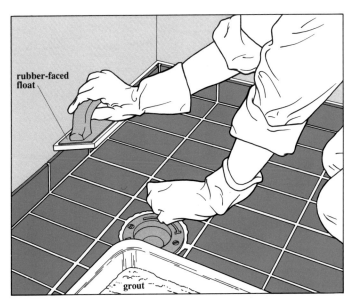

rubber-faced float

grout

6 **Grouting the tiles.** With a rubber-faced float, spread grout generously over the tiles, including trim tiles, as described on page 84, Step 17. Then press grout into the spaces between the wall and the trim tiles. Smooth grout over the top edge of the trim tile as well *(above)*. If you are using bullnose trim pieces — whose rounded top edges lie flat against the wall — do not smooth grout over the tops. Brushing diagonally, scrape off excess grout. Then clean the tiles with a sponge and clear water. Let the grout dry for 30 minutes before walking on it, but allow at least 24 hours for it to cure. Then wash the tiles with detergent. Have the plumber reinstall the toilet.

Extra storage
for a crowded room

Even the smallest of bathrooms usually houses linens, cleaning supplies, medicines, toiletries — perhaps even reading material. Mounting the washbasin in a vanity or chest of drawers *(pages 42-51)* meets many storage needs. For the rest, the cleverest answer is to add unobtrusive storage units to unused areas of the room. Recessing a mirrored medicine cabinet between wall studs, for example, takes advantage of invisible space *(pages 96-101)*. The neglected wall above the toilet can be exploited for shelves *(pages 92-95)*. And clear acrylic plastic can easily be crafted into a number of useful items, as shown in the collection at far right.

Plastics suppliers sell colored as well as clear acrylic. The colored versions — either tinted or opaque — hide scratches and blemishes better, but they are more expensive. Acrylics are available in 4-by-8-foot sheets and in cut-to-size pieces. The storage units here all are made from rectangles that you can cut accurately with a fine-toothed crosscut saw.

To protect the plastic's surfaces, both the top and bottom come wrapped in adhesive paper. Saw cuts are taken through it and the paper left intact until the plastic is read[?] to be bent. Then a narrow band of the protective paper pulled away and the exposed acrylic is heated over a hom[?] made strip heater *(below)* until it softens and bends freel[?] A double shelf, a magazine rack or a table is formed by tw[?] right-angled bends; a single shelf requires only a sing[?] bend. All work is done in a well-ventilated area to preve[?] accumulation of fumes from the heating plastic.

In order to overcome the acrylic's "memory" — its na[?] ural tendency to revert to its original form as it cools — th[?] bends are made slightly more than 90°, then fixed at t[?] desired angle by bracing the cooling acrylic against a 2-b[?] 4 *(Step 3)*. If the bend turns out wrong, the acrylic's mem[?] ory can be used to advantage: Reheat the piece, let it co[?] and flatten some — then bend it again.

To avoid chipping, mounting holes are drilled with twi[?] bits made for plastics. The only maintenance required [?] keep the acrylic clear is a periodic cleaning with mild soa[?] tepid water and a soft flannel rag. Do not use alcohol, pai[?] thinner or ammonia-based products such as window clea[?] er: They will mar the surface.

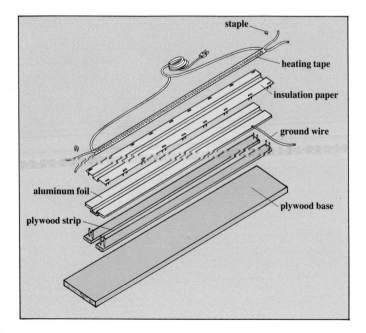

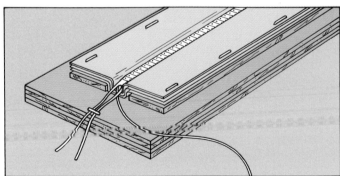

A homemade strip heater. The heater for bending acrylic is a layering of wood, insulation and heating tape, shown stacked at left and assembled above. Two 2½-by-36-inch strips of ¼-inch plywood are nailed, ¾ inch apart, to a 6-by-42-inch base of ½-inch plywood. Covering the wood are two layers of 6-by-36-inch heavy-duty aluminum foil and a 6-by-36-inch strip of insulation paper, such as Fluorglas® fiberglass-and-Teflon® tape. (The paper and heating tape are available where plastics are sold.) The foil is pierced by a screw for a ground wire, which connects to the cover-plate screw on an electrical outlet to prevent shock. Both foil and paper are pressed flat and stapled to the wood. The heating tape fits in the resulting trough, its strings stretched tight and stapled down.

Handy acrylic accessories. The storage accessories below all start as rectangles of clear acrylic. Dimensions can be modified as needed. Here, the rectangle for the double shelf is 24 by 36 inches; the single shelf, 10 by 24; the magazine rack, 9 by 24; the table, 14 by 36. Each piece is bent with a strip heater *(opposite);* mounting holes are made with a power drill *(overleaf).*

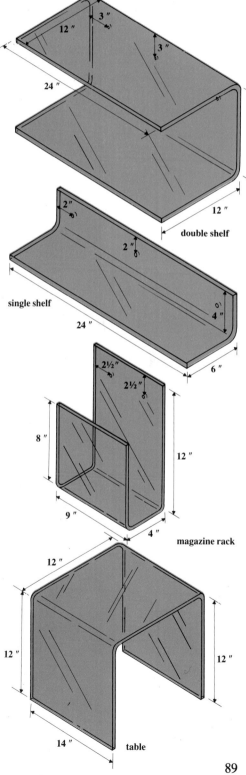

double shelf

single shelf

magazine rack

table

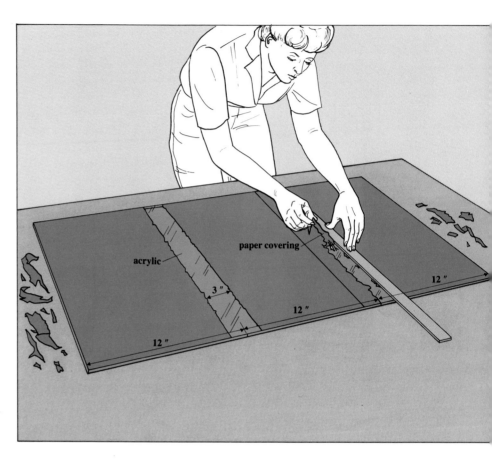

1 **Marking bend lines.** With its protective paper on, lay a piece of acrylic plastic — in this case a 36-by-24-inch rectangle — on a worktable. With a felt-tipped pen or grease pencil, mark the ends of each bend line by placing a tick on the long edge of the acrylic; for the double shelf shown in this demonstration, make two pairs of tick marks 12 inches from each short edge. Using a straightedge, draw lines across the paper to connect each pair of marks. Then draw parallel lines 1½ inches to either side of both of the bend lines. Remove the paper within these 3-inch-wide bands by starting a small tear at each line with your fingernail and tearing the paper along a straightedge *(above)*. Turn the acrylic over and strip the back side in the same way.

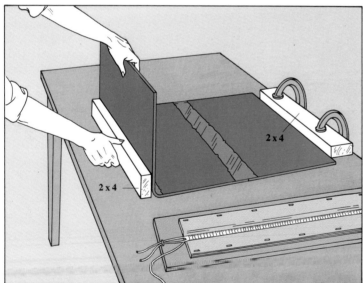

3 **Fixing the bend.** Unplug the strip heater and move it out of the way. Brace the unbent end of the acrylic against the 2-by-4. Press the wide side of another 2-by-4 against the back of the bend *(above)*. Hold the board steady for three minutes or until the acrylic is cool to the touch. The bend will be fixed at a 90° angle. If the bend turns out wrong, put the acrylic back over the strip heater and reheat the bend line. Repeat Step 2 and this step to form the second bend, positioning the strip heater along the edge of the worktable so that the formed shelf can hang over the table during the heating process.

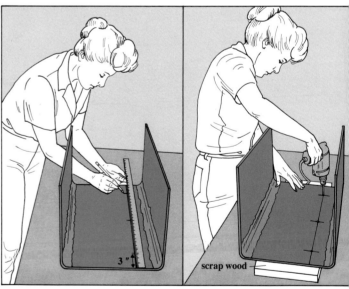

4 **Drilling mounting holes.** Lay the acrylic on its back, shelves upward. With a pencil and straightedge, draw a line on the protective paper 3 inches from the tick marks for one of the shelves. Make tick marks along the line 3 inches from each side and at the center *(above, left)*. Put the acrylic on a large piece of scrap wood. Fit a power drill with a ³⁄₁₆-inch twist bit for plastics, and drill through the marks *(above, right)*.

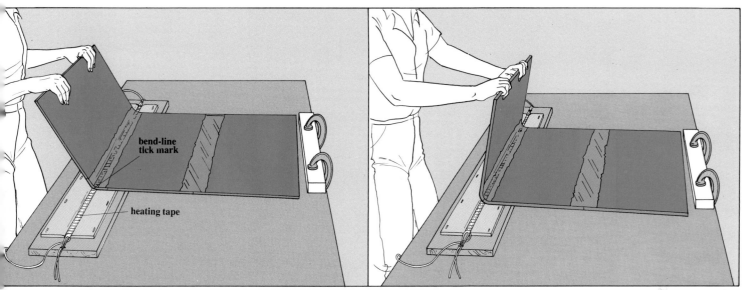

2 **Heating a bend.** Clamp both ends of a 2-by-4 to the far side of the table to provide a brace against which the acrylic can be propped after the bend is heated. Assemble a strip heater and plug it in. Grasp one end of the acrylic sheet with both hands, thumbs against the bottom side. Hold the sheet over the heater so that one pair of bend-line tick marks is centered over the heating tape. To avoid singeing, make sure that the acrylic does not actually touch the tape. Heat the bend line evenly, testing the acrylic frequently for pliancy by gently lifting the end of the sheet *(above, left)* and dropping it. Turn the acrylic over repeatedly so that both sides of the bend line are heated. Continue heating until the acrylic begins to droop slightly at the bend line — usually after about five to seven minutes. Then, slowly and evenly, bend the acrylic along the bend line until the endpiece is slightly beyond perpendicular *(above, right).*

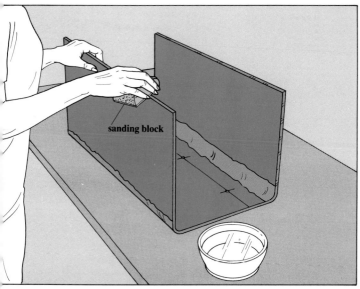

5 **Finishing the acrylic.** Wipe away the bend-line marks with a paper towel. Make a sanding block by wrapping a quarter sheet of medium (100-grit) sandpaper around a block of wood measuring about 1 by 2 by 4 inches. Holding the acrylic with one hand, sand the edges until the rough cut marks disappear. Repeat with pieces of very fine (220-grit) and extra-fine (320-grit) wet-and-dry sandpaper, dunking the block frequently in a dish of water as you work, until the edges are clear.

6 **Mounting the shelf.** Rather than mixing stud and hollow-wall fasteners, locate the studs in the wall on which you plan to hang the shelf *(page 124)*, then position the shelf against the wall, making sure all three marks miss the studs. Insert a pencil through each hole in the shelf to mark screw-hole positions. Set the shelf down and fit a power drill with a 5/16-inch bit. Drill at the marks and insert a plastic screw anchor for a No. 8 self-tapping screw into each wall hole. Strip all of the protective paper from the shelf. Pressing the shelf to the wall, drive a No. 8 self-tapping screw, with chrome finish washer, into the anchor in the center hole. Repeat for the other holes and tighten all three screws.

Space-saving bathroom shelves

Small rooms demand ingenious solutions to the problem of where put things; the wall-mounted she unit shown at left takes clever advantage of the normally unused are above the toilet. Four adjustable shelve suspended from metal tracks attached the sidepieces, provide convenient stor age for soaps, towels and other amenitie Below the shelves, the tilted platform the serves as a handy magazine rack will l out to allow access to the toilet tank.

All of the shelf's components exce the hardwood lower mounting cleat a made of ¾-inch AA-quality oak-vene plywood; one 4-by-8-foot sheet is amp You can also use dimensioned lumber – pine, redwood or cedar — or an A2-gra birch plywood. Have your lumber deal cut the pieces specified in the Materia List *(right),* or cut them yourself on a t ble saw. Metal shelf tracking is sold lengths of 3, 4, 5 and 6 feet; buy four foot lengths and trim them into strips a proximately 40 inches long *(Step 4).*

The shelf unit shown here is 84 inch high and 26½ inches wide overall, but interior width is just 25 inches, allowi the uprights and the magazine-shelf lip clear the sides and top of the toilet tank at least 2½ inches. To maintain simil margins around a tank that is wider th 20 inches, increase the length of the ho zontal pieces by an equivalent amoun similarly, to accommodate a tank tall than 28 inches, position the lower moun ing cleat and magazine shelf farther fro the bottom by the same amount when y mark the sidepieces *(Step 1).*

Building the shelves calls for only a fe simple tools: a hacksaw, a half-round fi corner clamps, and a drill equipped with variety of twist bits. You will also nee a carpenter's square and a saber saw cut baseboard notches in the unit's sid pieces, and a carpenter's level to moun the unit against the wall.

After you have assembled the she cover the exposed plywood edges wi iron-on oak-veneer edge banding; tri the edges of the banding with the fin toothed face of a file. Fill in the scre holes with wood putty, then smooth t surfaces with fine (150-grit) sandpape For the oak-veneer plywood shown, fi ish the pieces with two or three coats polyurethane varnish, rubbing the su face with extra fine (3/0) steel wool b tween coats. For painted shelves, se

...e wood surface with an enamel under-
...oat, and brush on two or three coats of
...l-based enamel.

...Mount the shelf against the wall with
...crews driven into wall anchors (*Step 8*).
...aution: Before drilling mounting holes
...bove the toilet, turn off the electricity to
...e bathroom and adjacent rooms at the
...rvice panel. If you hit a pipe when drill-
...g, turn off the main water supply imme-
...ately and call a plumber.

Materials List

Plywood	1 sheet AA-quality ¾ ″ oak-veneer plywood, 4 ′ x 8 ′, cut into: 2 sidepieces, 8 ″ x 84 ″ 1 top piece, 8 ″ x 25 ″ 1 upper mounting cleat, 1½ ″ x 25 ″ 1 shelf cleat, 1½ ″ x 24¾ ″ 1 magazine-shelf lip, 1½ ″ x 24¾ ″ 1 magazine shelf, 12 ″ x 24¾ ″ 2 magazine-shelf supports, 1½ ″ x 7 ″ 4 shelves, 8 ″ x 24½ ″
Hardwood	1 lower mounting cleat, 1¾ ″ x 1¾ ″ x 25 ″
Edge banding	¾ ″ iron-on oak-veneer edge banding, 30 ′ long
Hardware	4 lengths brass-finish shelving track, 48 ″ long, with nails 16 brass-finish pin brackets 8 oz. threepenny finishing nails 12 No. 8 flat-head wood screws, 1½ ″ long 2 No. 8 flat-head wood screws, 2 ″ long 2 No. 8 flat-head wood screws, 2½ ″ long 4 plastic wall anchors for No. 8 wood screws

...bove-the-toilet shelves. The shelf frame
...onsists of two sides, a top and a pair of
...ounting cleats. Four adjustable shelves
...e suspended on pin brackets from metal
...elf tracks attached to the sidepieces
...ith nails. The removable magazine shelf
...sts on supports that are nailed diagonal-
...· to the sidepieces; a plywood cleat attached
...· the back of the shelf holds it in place.
...he shelf supports, magazine-shelf lip and
...elf cleat are secured with threepenny
...nishing nails; all other joints are secured
...ith No. 8 flat-head wood screws. The
...xposed edges of all the pieces are covered
...ith iron-on oak-veneer edge banding,
...nd the unit is mounted against the wall with
...o. 8 screws in counterbored holes
...rilled through the upper and lower cleats.

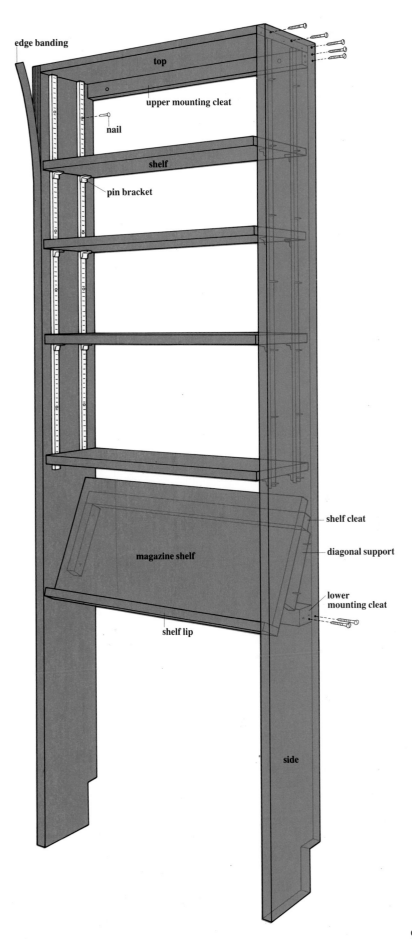

edge banding

top

upper mounting cleat

nail

shelf

pin bracket

shelf cleat

diagonal support

magazine shelf

lower mounting cleat

shelf lip

side

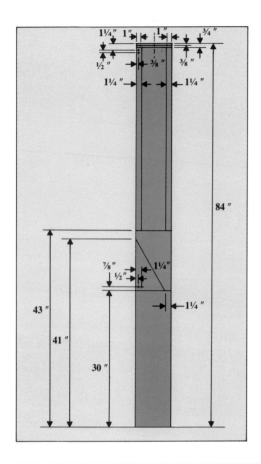

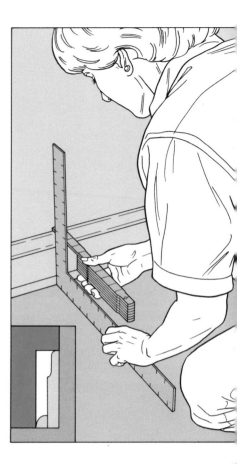

1 **Marking the sidepieces.** Label the front, back and bottom edges of one 84-inch-long sidepiece. Draw magazine-shelf guidelines on the inner face 30 and 43 inches from the bottom; mark the back edge 41 inches from the bottom. Make a mark 1¼ inches from the front edge on the 30-inch line. Draw a diagonal line connecting that mark with the 41-inch mark on the back edge.

Draw shelf-track guidelines — one ¾ inch from the top, two starting from that line and extending perpendicular to it, 1¼ inches from the front and back edges, as far as the line 43 inches from the bottom.

Mark screw holes for the shelf top and the mounting cleats on the board's edges, as shown at left. Mark the other sidepiece the same way, but reverse the diagonal line so that the second board mirrors the first.

2 **Cutting baseboard notches.** Set a carpenter's square flush against the floor molding behind the toilet. Hold a ruler, its tip against the wall just above the baseboard, perpendicular to the square's vertical leg. Read the height of the molding from the square and the thickness of the molding from the ruler.

Draw a rectangle of these dimensions on the bottom back corner of each sidepiece. Then use a saber saw to cut out each rectangular notch with two cuts, starting both at the outside edge of the board. Each notch should fit neatly over the baseboard and floor molding (inset).

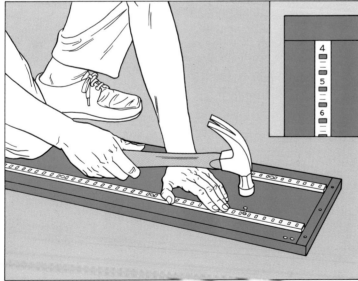

lower mounting cleat

5 **Attaching shelving track to sidepieces.** Find the stamped numeral at one end of a 48-inch-long strip of metal shelving track. With the tip of an awl, mark the edge of the track beside the hole that is nearest to — but not more than — 40 inches from the numeral. (Cutting the track at a hole requires the least effort.) Cut the track at the mark with a hacksaw; then cut three more pieces the same length. Now align strips of track inside the two vertical lines of one sidepiece so their ends just touch the horizontal line at the top of the board. Secure the tracks to the board with the nails provided by the track manufacturer; fasten the top and bottom ends of tracks first, then space the nails at 5-inch intervals (above). Attach the other two tracks to the other sidepiece the same way.

6 **Assembling the frame.** Set the sidepieces and shelf top on edge on the floor, and clamp them together with two corner clamps. Use a drill fitted with a 3/32-inch twist bit to bore pilot holes into the ends of the top through the holes in the sidepieces. Remove the clamps and apply glue to the ends of the top, reposition it between the sidepieces and secure the joints with 1½-inch No. 8 screws. Position the upper and lower mounting cleats between the sidepieces and drill pilot holes into their ends through the sidepiece holes the same way. Apply glue to the top lo edge and ends of the upper cleat; position it flush against the underside of the top and attach it to the sidepieces with screws. Finally, glue the ends of the lower cleat and attach it to the sidepieces similarly.

3 **Attaching shelf supports to sidepieces.** Make a pencil mark at the exact center of the long diagonal line on one sidepiece. Mark the center of one long edge of a shelf support. Apply a thin ribbon of yellow carpenter's glue to one face of the support and position it glued side down on the diagonal line of the sidepiece, aligning the center marks. Secure the pieces together with two threepenny finishing nails, spaced 1½ inches from each end of the support *(above)*. Attach the other shelf support to the other sidepiece with glue and nails the same way.

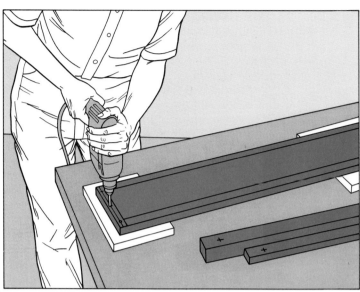

4 **Drilling counterbored screw holes.** Lay one sidepiece on the work surface, marked side up, with a scrap supporting the ends and middle. Using a drill fitted with a ³⁄₁₆-inch twist bit, bore screw-shank holes all the way through the marked locations on the board's top and back edges *(above)*. Then turn the board over and use a ³⁄₈-inch twist bit to bore ¼-inch-deep counterbore holes in each shank hole; tape the bit ¼ inch from the tip to gauge the depth of the hole. Drill counterbored holes in the other sidepiece similarly. Finally, mark the center of the faces of the upper and lower mounting cleats 2 inches from each end; drill counterbored holes through the marks in the cleats the same way.

7 **Attaching lip and cleat to magazine shelf.** Lay the shelf lip on the work surface and start, but do not drive in, three threepenny nails ³⁄₈ inch from one long edge; place the nails 1 inch from each end and in the middle. Apply glue to one long edge of the magazine shelf, then set the lip on edge abutting the shelf and drive in the nails *(above)*. Turn the shelf over and draw a line 3 inches from, and parallel to, the long edge opposite the shelf lip. Apply glue to one face of the shelf cleat and position it glued side down along the line *(inset)*. Secure the pieces with three threepenny nails placed 1 inch from each end and in the middle.

When installed, the magazine shelf rests on the two diagonal supports and is held in place by its cleat sitting atop the supports' ends.

8 **Mounting the shelves.** Set the shelf frame upright against the wall behind the toilet and center it over the tank. Hold a carpenter's level against one sidepiece *(above)*, then adjust the position of the frame until it is level. Use an awl to make punch marks in the wall through the holes in both cleats. Remove the frame, then use a drill fitted with the appropriate bit for your wall anchor to bore 1½-inch-deep holes at the top punch marks and 1-inch-deep holes at the bottom marks. Drive the wall anchors into the holes, reposition the frame against the wall and secure it with four No. 8 screws; use 2-inch screws in the upper mounting cleat, 2½-inch screws in the lower cleat. Finally, attach iron-on edge banding to all exposed plywood edges and install the shelves.

A capacious cabinet built into the wall

Inside a bathroom, where every inch of space is precious, hiding a home-built medicine cabinet within a wall solves several problems at once. The recessed chest — such as the 40-by-23½-by-5½-inch version shown below — can be larger and deeper than factory-made models. Its mirror, housed in a stainless-steel picture frame, can be bigger and brighter. And unlike surface-mounted cabinets, a built-in chest can be set behind the basin, so you can wash your face without bumping the mirror.

However, constructing a recessed cabinet requires cutting a hole in the wall and removing sections of one or two studs, then patching the wall. These procedures are easy enough for amateurs to accomplish when the wall is sheathed with wallboard, but should be left to professionals when the wall is plaster, paneling or tile. Removing one or two studs from most interior walls is safe, but consult an architect or a structural engineer before building a cabinet in an exterior wall or in a structurally important interior wall, usually recognizable because it runs across the house, perpendicular to the floor joists (often visible from the basement) and rafters.

You also must avoid plumbing pipes and electric wires. Before cutting into a wall, study the placement of fixtures and outlets on the floors above and below. Turn on nearby faucets and listen at the wall; cancel your plans if you hear running water. Always cut into the wall cautiously, so that damage will be minimized if you encounter unexpected obstacles.

Ideally the cabinet should be centered over a washbasin, near an electrical receptacle and a good light source, with the exposed cabinet hinge on the least conspicuous side. If a stud falls near the planned cabinet's edge, you may want to nail one side of the cabinet to the stud, simplifying both the cabinet's construction and later wallboard repairs.

If the studs are 24 inches apart, you may want to fit a slightly narrower 22½-inch cabinet between two studs, rather than removing a stud. If you find you must remove a stud that supports a wallboard joint on the wall's other side, reinforce the joint by using ½-inch plywood for the cabinet's back; fasten the wallboard to the plywood with short screws. Be prepared to use shims (wedge-shaped shingles) as spacers to make the cabinet's parts fit squarely.

The cabinet's joinery also depends on care in choosing and fitting its wood parts. At the lumberyard insist on perfect boards, eyeballing each piece for warping. When assembling the cabinet, cut all of the boards squarely, with a miter box wide enough to handle 5½-inch stock or with a table saw or radial-arm saw.

Because the inner dimensions of picture frames vary according to manufacturer, buy the mirror first. When you order it ask for safety backing, which seals against moisture's corrosive effects and shatterproofs the glass. After the frame shop cuts a metal frame to fit the mirror, you can calculate the cabinet's exact size. Its height should be that of the frame, while its width should be ¼ inch less than the frame's width.

To repair the wall around the cabinet neatly, fit the wallboard itself rather loosely *(Step 11),* to avoid crumbling the edges; wallboard tape and joint compound will fill gaps as wide as ¼ inch. Taping, feathering and sanding the joint *(Steps 12-13)* requires care; do not scuff the wallboard's paper surface or expose the joint tape. Minor oversanding can be repaired by sponging scuffed areas with joint compound thinned with water. Before priming and painting the cabinet, vacuum-clean the wallboard, putty nail holes and fill cracks with latex caulk. Smooth the caulking bead with a damp rag and then with a bare finger.

Materials List

Picture frame	1 "-deep metal picture frame, about 40 " x 23½ ", with corner tabs and spring clips
Mirror	¼ " glass mirror with safety backing, 39¹³⁄₁₆ " x 23⁵⁄₁₆ "
Plywood	¼ " birch plywood mirror backing, 39¹³⁄₁₆ " x 23⁵⁄₁₆ "; ¼ " birch plywood back, 39¾ " x 23 "; 1 piece ⅜ "

plywood, 1½ " x 2 ", for strike block

Lumber	about 20 ' 2 x 4 framing lumber; about 12 ' clear pine 1 x 6, for cabinet and shelves; about 14 ' 1 x 2, for nailing cleats
Hardware	3 No. 8 wood screws, ½ " long; 1 magnetic latch with strike plate; 39 " continuous hinge; 20 No. 6 pan-head sheet-metal screws, ¼ " long; 20

No. 6 pan-head sheet-metal screws, ⅝ " long; 1 box ring-shanked wallboard nails, 1¼ " long; metal shelf brackets; fourpenny and sixpenny finishing nails; eightpenny and tenpenny common nails

Wallboard	1 piece wallboard, 4 ' x 4 '; 1 can ready-mixed joint compound; 1 roll perforated wallboard tape

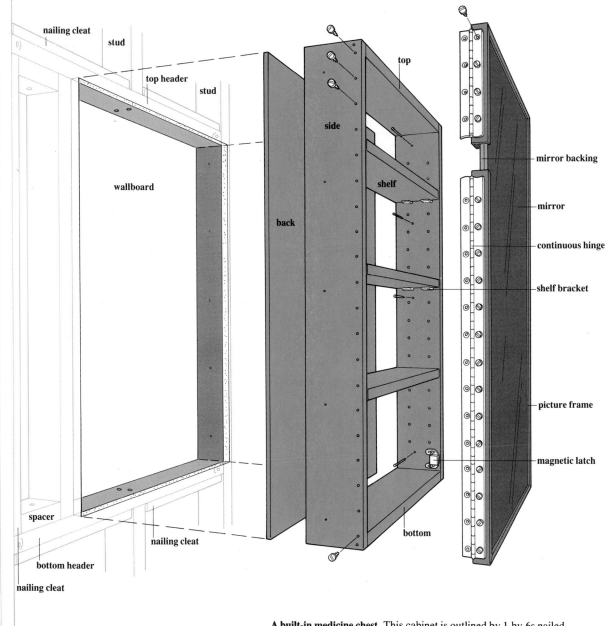

A built-in medicine chest. This cabinet is outlined by 1-by-6s nailed to a 2-by-4 framework of headers and uprights. The framework's 1-by-2 nailing cleats support wallboard patches. The cabinet itself has a plywood back. Adjustable shelves cut from 1-by-6 lumber rest on metal brackets, whose pins fit into holes drilled in each side of the cabinet. The cabinet's door, a metal picture frame that encloses a glass mirror, is mounted on a length of continuous hinge.

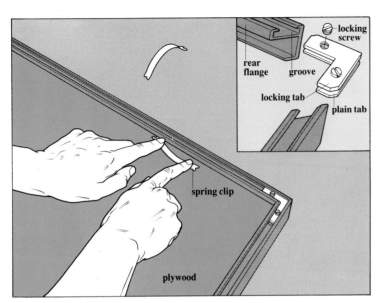

1 **Assembling the door.** Set a locking tab atop a matching plain tab at each end of the long sides of a metal picture frame of the required size (inset). Slide the two tabs together into the narrow rectangular groove along the frame's back and tighten the locking screw. Slide the frame's short sides onto the protruding tabs from one long side; tighten the locking screws for the short sides. Slide a precut piece of ¼-inch birch plywood into the frame, then slide the protruding tabs of the remaining long side into the matching grooves on the short sides and tighten the screws. To secure the plywood, insert the metal spring clips supplied with the frame between the plywood and the frame's rear flange (above).

2 **Marking the wall.** Find the studs behind the planned position of the new cabinet and to either side (page 124), and faintly mark their approximate locations on the wall with a pencil. Using a carpenter's level, draw a horizontal line for the cabinet's bottom 6 inches above the back splash and make bold cross marks 23¼ inches apart for the cabinet's sides. Have a helper align the door's bottom with the marks, then trace around the door's top corners (above). Set the door aside. Mark 1½ inches above each top corner and snap a horizontal chalk line that extends across the marks to the studs on each side; snap a similar line 1½ inches below the bottom corners. Use the level to extend the vertical marks for the outside of the cabinet below this horizontal line.

5 **Cutting the studs.** With a combination square draw horizontal lines level with the bottom of the opening across the edge and faces of each intermediate stud. Draw matching lines across the studs 43 inches above the first ones. Use a backsaw or a crosscut saw to cut each stud along each set of lines (above), then pull out the severed section of stud and any attached firestops. Pull any remaining nails from studs or firestops with a claw hammer and cut off exposed nail tips with carpenter's nippers or end-cutting pliers.

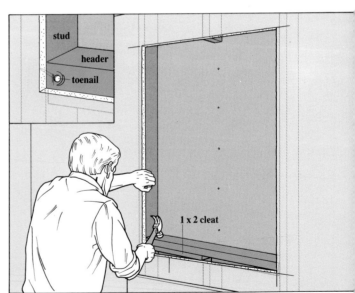

6 **Nailing the headers.** Cut a 2-by-4 that fits snugly between the outside studs at the opening's bottom. To support the old wallboard below the opening, nail 1-by-2 cleats to one face of the 2-by-4, leaving gaps between cleats for any intermediate studs. Tap this 2-by-4 header into place, cleats downward (above). Fasten it to each intermediate stud with tenpenny nails. Level the header and mark its ends on the outside studs. Tap the point of an eightpenny nail straight into the header's edge about ¾ inch from one end, then angle the nail sideways and drive (or toenail) it through the header's end into the stud (inset). Toenail the header's other end to its stud. Mark lines across the studs 40 inches above the bottom header, then nail a matching top header above the line

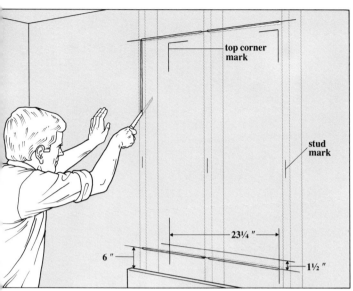

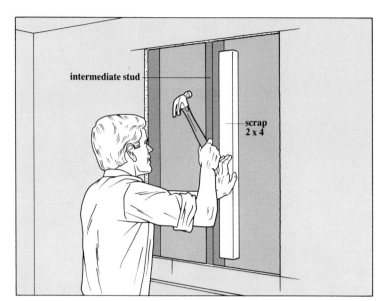

3 **Removing the wallboard.** Set the point of a wallboard saw between studs on the lower chalk line and tap on the butt of the saw handle with a hammer until the blade breaks through the wallboard. Saw along the chalk line, restarting the saw on the opposite side of any intermediate studs. In the same way, saw along the top chalk line and vertically along the inside edges of the two outer studs (above), using each stud's edge as a guide. Then break the cutout rectangle of wallboard into pieces with a hammer and tear out the pieces by hand. With a claw hammer pry away fragments clinging to intermediate studs and to firestops — 2-by-4 crosspieces set between studs about 4 feet above the floor.

4 **Freeing the intermediate studs.** Hold a scrap of 2-by-4 about 2 feet long flat against the exposed underside of the wallboard or paneling in the room behind the opening. Set the edge of the 2-by-4 against one face of an intermediate stud and strike the 2-by-4's face smartly once with a hammer (above) to pop free the nailheads that fasten the wall surface to the stud or to horizontal firestops, if any. Working on the wall in the room behind the opening, drive the popped nails opposite the opening clear through the wallboard or paneling with a hammer and a nail set. Then secure the wallboard above and below the opening by resetting any nailheads that were popped free.

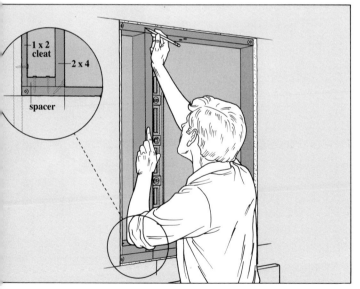

7 **Framing one side.** Transfer the mark made in Step 2 for what will be the hinge side of the cabinet from the wallboard to the bottom header. If the mark is 2¼ inches or less from the outside stud, nail to the stud long strips of plywood or lumber that sum to the needed thickness. For wider gaps, first nail a 1-by-2 cleat to the stud; cut a 2-by-4 to fit snugly between the headers and set it in place, aligning its inner face with the mark. Cut a spacer from a 2-by-4 or plywood to fit horizontally between the cleat and the 2-by-4. Then nail both the spacer and the 2-by-4 to the bottom header (inset). Using a level, adjust the 2-by-4 until it is vertical. Mark its top end on the header (above). Nail a spacer between the 2-by-4's top and the cleat, then toenail the 2-by-4 to the header.

8 **Gluing the back.** Mark the top and bottom headers 23¼ inches from the vertical 2-by-4 installed in the preceding step. Between this mark and the adjacent outside stud install a vertical 2-by-4, a 1-by-2 cleat and any necessary spacers. Cut a piece of birch plywood ¼ inch smaller in each dimension than the framed opening. Use ½-inch plywood if any of the studs removed in Step 5 supported a wallboard joint on the wall's reverse side; otherwise use ¼-inch plywood. With a caulking gun apply a zigzag bead of panel adhesive to the paper backing of the wallboard that is exposed within the framed opening. Then press the plywood back firmly into the panel adhesive (above). ▶

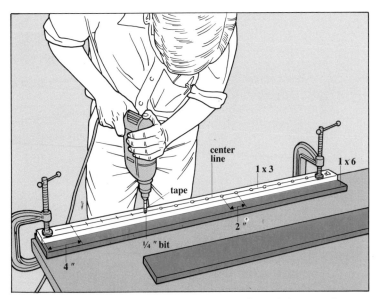

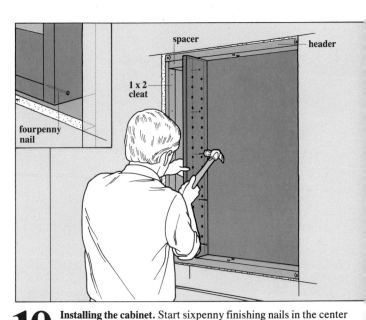

9 **Drilling for shelf brackets.** Cut two 1-by-6s to fit snugly between the headers. Cut a scrap 1-by-3 of the same length, snap a chalk line along its center line and label one end as its bottom. Starting 4 inches from the bottom, mark across the center line every 2 inches. Clamp the 1-by-3 to the face of one 1-by-6, aligning the edges and bottom ends. Fit a drill with a ¼-inch bit and wrap tape around the bit 1⅛ inches from its tip. Along the 1-by-3's center line, at each mark, drill into the boards until the tape barely touches the 1-by-3. Use the same jig to drill matching holes near the 1-by-6's other edge and in the second 1-by-6.

10 **Installing the cabinet.** Start sixpenny finishing nails in the center of each 1-by-6 every 6 inches or so, beginning 3 inches from the bottom. Set each 1-by-6 between the headers, with its rear edge tight against the plywood and its back against the vertical 2-by-4 frame; drive the nails home into the 2-by-4 (*above*).

Cut 1-by-6s to fit horizontally between the tops and bottoms of the vertical pieces and fasten them to the headers with sixpenny finishing nails. To lock each corner together, near the cabinet's front edge drive a fourpenny finishing nail through the vertical 1-by-6 into the horizontal one (*inset*).

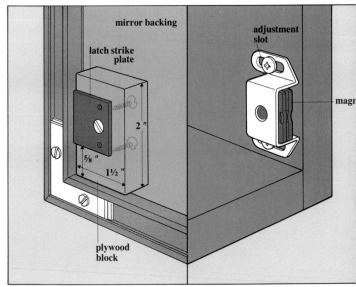

13 **Feathering the edges.** Using a 6- or 8-inch wallboard knife, coat the tape with a ⅛-inch-deep bed of joint compound. Then hold the bare knife over one edge of the tape, with the knife's edge barely overlapping the tape's width, and remove excess compound by drawing the knife along the tape (*above*) while applying fractionally greater pressure on the knife-edge farthest from the joint. Feather the other edge similarly, making sure the tape remains completely covered with compound. Cover nailheads and dents with joint compound and let the compound dry for 24 hours. Apply a final coat of compound to the joints and nailheads similarly, then smooth it with a sanding block and medium (100-grit) paper.

14 **Installing the latch.** At the corner of the frame that will hold the latch (*above, left*), set a 1½-by-2-inch block of ½-inch plywood against the rear surface of the plywood mirror backing, with the block's edges aligned with the frame's rear flange. Fasten the backing to the block with glue and two No. 8 wood screws ½ inch long. Place the latch's metal strike plate vertically on the block, its bottom edge ⅝ inch from the block's bottom edge, and fasten the plate with another screw. Hold the magnetic latch to the bottom of the cabinet's matching side, aligning the magnet with the cabinet's front edge, and secure it with screws (*above, right*). Unfasten the frame's hinge-side piece and remove it.

11 **Patching the wallboard.** On a new piece of wallboard, mark a rectangle ⅛ inch smaller in both dimensions than each wall opening, using the board's manufactured edges for two sides of the rectangle. Cut along the shorter line with a wallboard saw, then score deeply along the longer line with a utility knife *(above)*; if the rectangle is less than 2 inches wide, also score the board's reverse side. Set the scored line atop the table edge and press the rectangle down until the board snaps. Cut the backing paper behind the break. Fasten the patch to the framing with 1¼-inch wallboard nails spaced 8 inches apart, driving the nails home until the hammer's head just makes a dimple in the patch, without tearing its paper face.

utility knife

12 **Taping the joints.** Butter a 4-inch broad knife with ready-mixed joint compound. Fill each joint by drawing the knife steadily along it while decreasing the blade's angle. Scrape away excess compound and let the joint dry for 24 hours. Then spread a ¼-inch-deep bed of compound over the joint. At the joint's end, press a strip of perforated wallboard tape into the compound, then draw the knife along the tape *(above)* while pressing firmly enough to squeeze out excess compound, leaving a ⅛-inch thickness of tape and compound. Lightly pass the knife over the tape once again to smooth out bubbles and wrinkles, but do not try to eliminate minor waviness, which will disappear as the tape dries.

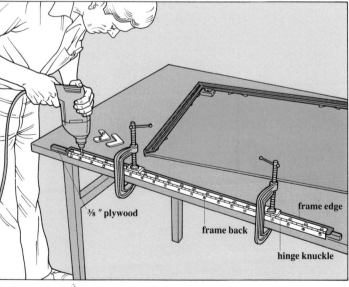

⅜″ plywood
frame edge
frame back
hinge knuckle

15 **Attaching the hinge.** Put the frame's long piece on a worktable, its edge facing upward and a scrap of ⅜-inch plywood supporting the overhanging lip. Fold a 39-inch continuous hinge into a right angle and center one leaf on the frame piece's edge, with the other leaf held against the piece's back and the hinge knuckle pointing outward. Secure hinge and frame to the table with C clamps. Through the hinge's holes, drill ³⁄₃₂-inch holes in the frame *(above)*; then fasten the hinge to the frame with ¼-inch No. 6 pan-head sheet-metal screws. Paint the plywood mirror backing, the wallboard and the cabinet. Slide the plywood and the mirror together into the frame, add the hinged piece and replace the spring clips *(Step 1)*.

16 **Hanging the door.** Fit a drill with a ³⁄₃₂-inch twist bit and wrap tape around the bit ½ inch from its tip. Open the door's hinge flat. Have a helper hold the picture frame against the cabinet while you align their top and bottom edges. Then drill through two of the hinge's holes into the top and bottom of the cabinet, stopping when the tape reaches the hinge. Drive ⅝-inch-long No. 6 pan-head sheet-metal screws into these holes *(above)*, then drill through the remaining hinge holes and drive screws through them. Cut 1-by-6 shelves 21¾ inches long, then paint them and install them inside the cabinet on metal shelf brackets.

Amenities: The finishing touch

However sophisticated its design, a bathroom needs amenities—those small appointments combining practical convenience and decorative pleasure—to make it a personal and hospitable place. This chapter contains projects to help achieve that end: a portable towel rack (*pages 104-107*); a tray that fits across the tub and holds bathing essentials (*pages 108-111*); a custom-sewed shower curtain and a skirt to hide pipes under the basin (*pages 112-117*); mirrored doors for a built-in tub and shower (*pages 118-120*). In addition every bathroom welcomes factory-made fripperies like those shown here. The best are made from rustproof materials such as plastic, brass or stainless steel; avoid fittings of ordinary steel, which may rust regardless of their coating.

To mount the hardware, you often must drill neat holes through ceramic tile, a brittle, breakable material whose slippery glaze sends drill bits skittering. Start such holes by marking the glaze with a nail set or center punch and a hammer, then use a carbide-tipped masonry bit to drill slowly through the tile. To seal out water, thoroughly fill the fitting's hollow back (if any) with silicone caulk, and caulk around the holes; then drive the screws home.

Bathroom fittings generally have two basic fastening systems. Hardware can be fastened directly to the wall studs with long screws (*below*), the strongest possible method. An alternate system uses a mounting bracket that is screwed to the wall. The fitting then locks over the bracket and, in some cases, is secured with a setscrew (*opposite*); both arrangements hide the screws but allow easy removal of the fitting. In all systems the fasteners supplied with the hardware often prove inadequate—particularly when a mounting plate is located between studs. If you cannot fasten the fitting directly to the wall's wood framework with screws, use fasteners that expand behind the wall covering—toggle bolts, for example. Avoid plastic or lead anchors, which gradually loosen with hard wear.

Hardware around a tub or shower, such as the towel bar below, requires especially careful mounting: If someone slips in the bath, the nearest projection perforce becomes a grab bar. Ideally two full-fledged horizontal grab bars 1 inches in diameter should be installed above a tub, 24 and 56 inches off the floor. Each bar should be fastened to the wall studs with No. 10 wood screws 3½ inches long, which are capable of supporting a 250-pound load. To match an extra-long bar to the existing stud spacing, shorten the bar with a hacksaw or a pipe cutter.

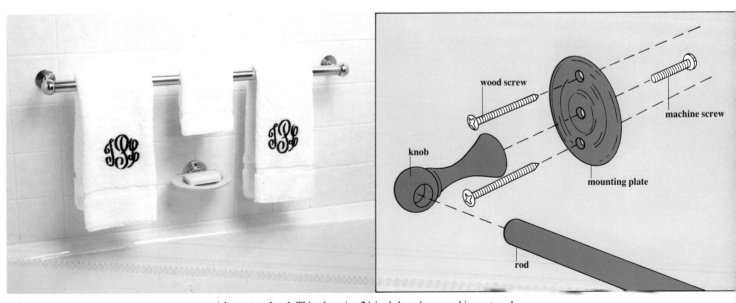

A brass towel rod. This gleaming 24-inch-long brass rod is centered alongside the tub, 24 inches above the floor. The rod's ends are housed in the cylindrical recesses of solid brass knobs. Each mounting plate is fastened to a knob with a machine screw, then anchored to a wall stud with 2-inch brass oval-head wood screws — in this case, Phillips™ screws. The one-piece brass-and-ceramic soap dish has a simpler mounting system, merely requiring two wood screws that run through its backplate and the ceramic tile into a stud.

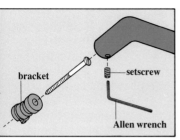

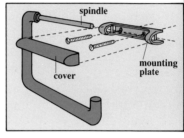

A one-piece towel rod. This U-shaped nylon towel rod's sleek lines are uninterrupted by hidden mounting hardware, which is equally adaptable to a bathroom door (*above*) or to a wall. At each end of the rod, a plug-shaped mounting bracket is fastened to the wall with a single screw. Matching sockets within the rod's ends fit over the brackets and are anchored by setscrews that are tightened with an Allen wrench, usually supplied with the rod.

A versatile plastic holder. This colorful C-shaped plastic holder elegantly accommodates either a hand towel or a roll of toilet paper. Screws fasten the holder's mounting plate to the wall. The C's upper arm is a spindle that slides through channels in the mounting plate and is then secured by the plate's snap-on cover.

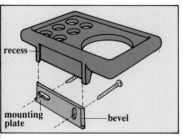

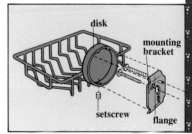

Washbasin niceties. Made of boldly colored plastic, these fittings can accommodate a tumbler and six toothbrushes, and a large bar of soap. Both fittings have identical mounting systems: A plastic mounting plate with beveled edges is screwed to the wall and an interlocking recess in the fixture's back slides down onto the plate.

A metal soap dish. This self-draining soap dish of brass wire, with a protective coating of white epoxy that preserves the wire's flexibility, hangs unobtrusively over a tub or washbasin. The dish's disk-shaped back conceals its mounting bracket. The bracket's angled flanges pull the disk snugly against the wall and a setscrew tightens the disk to the bracket from below; the bracket itself is fastened to the wall with screws.

A freestanding towel rack

The Shaker-inspired towel rack below is faithful to the economy of that early-19th Century design tradition, yet it is both sturdy enough to hold a bundle of wet bath towels and lightweight enough to be moved in front of a heat source to dry the towels.

The rack is made of six pieces of stock pine. The legs and bases are 1-by-2s and 1-by-3s connected by lap joints, formed by fitting a chiseled notch at the bottom of each leg into a matching notch in a base.

The bases are shaped with a saber saw.

The crossbars — two strips of ¾-inch-square molding stock — attach to the legs with wood screws. If you prefer round bars, drill ⅝-inch holes to fit ⅝-inch wood dowels, cut 25½ inches long so they will extend through the sidepieces.

As in any project, the elegance of the finished rack depends on accurate measuring — and sharp tools. Test the chisel and saber saw on scrap wood. If the chisel crushes or splits the wood rather than slicing smoothly, have it sharpened at hardware store. If the saw burns or splinters the wood, replace the blade.

Sand the rack with medium (100-grit) and fine (150-grit) paper to smooth the corners and give the rack a silky surface. Then seal the pine with primer, diluted one to one, sand it again and finish it with several coats of enamel. Or, if you prefer the look of natural wood, finish the rack with penetrating wood stain and polyurethane varnish or with a penetrating oil.

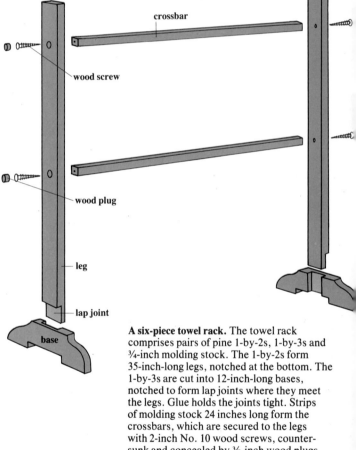

A six-piece towel rack. The towel rack comprises pairs of pine 1-by-2s, 1-by-3s and ¾-inch molding stock. The 1-by-2s form 35-inch-long legs, notched at the bottom. The 1-by-3s are cut into 12-inch-long bases, notched to form lap joints where they meet the legs. Glue holds the joints tight. Strips of molding stock 24 inches long form the crossbars, which are secured to the legs with 2-inch No. 10 wood screws, countersunk and concealed by ⅜-inch wood plugs.

Materials List

1 x 2	6 ′ clear pine 1 x 2, cut into 2 legs, 35 ″ long
1 x 3	2 ′ clear pine 1 x 3, cut into 2 base pieces, 12 ″ long
Molding stock	50 ″ ¾ ″-square molding stock, cut into 2 pieces, 24 ″ long
Wood plugs	4 ⅜ ″ wood plugs, ⅜ ″ long
Screws	4 No. 10 flat-head wood screws, 2 ″ long
Finish	alkyd primer undercoat oil-based semigloss enamel

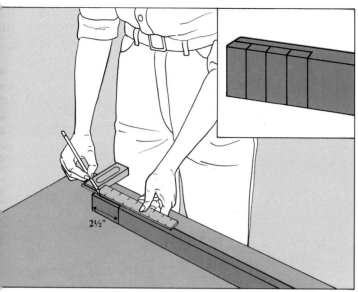

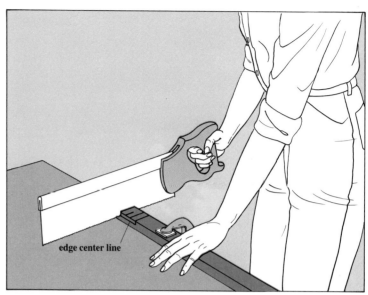

1 **Drawing notches on the legs.** Using a carpenter's square and a sharp pencil, draw a line across the face of a 1-by-2 leg, 2½ inches from one end. Continue the line across both edges of the 1-by-2. Turn the leg on edge and mark the midpoint of the edge line and the midpoint of the board's end. Connect these marks with a line *(above)*. Turn the board over and draw a similar line down the center of the other edge. Make three more lines across the face of the board, evenly spaced and parallel to the original line; extend these lines onto both edges as far as the center lines *(inset)*. Draw identical lines on one end of the second 1-by-2.

2 **Cutting the notches.** Set one leg at a time on a worktable, with its marked face up. Clamp the leg to the table, fitting a thin piece of scrap wood between the clamp and the leg to protect the surface of the leg. Then use a backsaw to cut through the four lines on the face of the leg, down to the center lines on the edges.

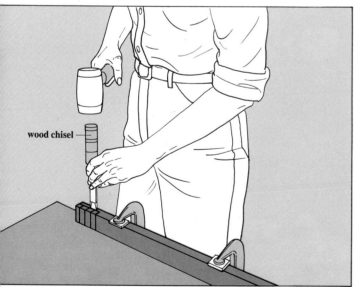

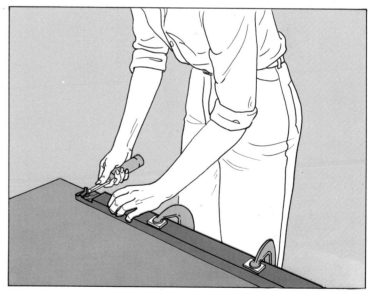

3 **Chiseling the notches.** Set one leg on its edge and clamp it to the worktable. Stand the blade of a ½-inch wood chisel — its beveled edge facing the sawed surface — at the inner end of the penciled center line. Make a shallow groove along the line by lightly tapping the top of the chisel with a mallet or hammer, moving the chisel as you go. Turn the piece over, clamp it in place, and make a similar groove along the center line on the other edge. Now work along the groove again, this time striking the top of the chisel with short, sharp taps of the mallet or hammer. Carefully chisel out the wood down to the middle of the board all the way along the groove. Then turn the leg over, reclamp it, and repeat the process along the opposite edge. Repeat for the second leg.

4 **Smoothing the notches.** Clamp one leg at a time flat on the worktable. Use the chisel, beveled edge up, to shave the notch, smoothing out the chiseled area until the notch is a flat surface even with the center lines on both sides of the leg. Be careful not to shave too deep and gouge the notch. Caution: When using the chisel to shave a flat surface, point the blade away from you, and keep your free hand out of its path. ▶

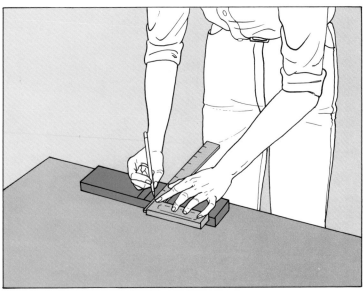

5 **Marking the base pieces.** Mark the midpoint of the length of one face of a 1-by-3 base piece. From that point, measure and mark a distance toward each end equal to one half the width of a leg (approximately ¾ inch). Use the carpenter's square to draw lines across the base piece, perpendicular to its edge, through each of the three marks (above). Continue the lines across both edges. Repeat for the second base piece.

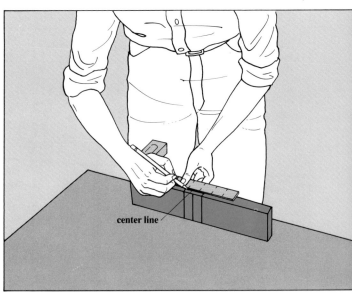

center line

6 **Marking the edges.** Mark the midpoints of the two outside edge lines and connect the marks by drawing a line down the center of the edge (above). Repeat for the opposite edge, then make similar marks on the second base piece. After marking both base pieces, saw halfway through each piece along the three parallel lines on its face, as in Step 2, then chisel and shave away the wood as in Steps 3 and 4.
TIP: Saw just inside the two outside lines so the notch in the base piece will be slightly narrower than the leg is wide. This will ensure a sn fit between the leg and the base piece.

9 **Tracing the pattern.** Set the lap-jointed assembly on the worktable, with the jointed face of the leg facing upward: This will be the inside surface of the leg when the rack is finished. Trace the pattern onto one side of the base. Flip the pattern over, move it to the opposite side of the base and repeat the tracing. Trace the pattern onto the second base piece.

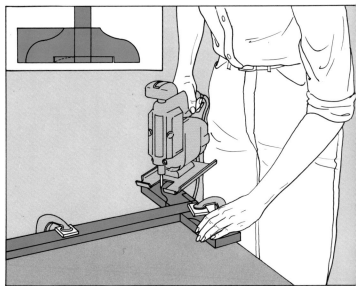

10 **Cutting out the base.** Clamp the assembly to the worktable, jointed side up, with half of the base hanging over the table's edge as shown above. Cut along the curved line with a saber saw. Reclamp the unit so the bottom of the base overhangs the edge. Start cutting out the bottom (inset) by sawing along the two vertical lines. Next, from just inside the left-hand cut, saw an arc (dotted line) from left to right up to the horizontal line. Then cut straight across to the right. Finally, cut into the left-hand corner from the right. Move the assembly to the other side of the table to cut the second set of curves in the base. Cut the base of the second leg, then smooth all newly cut surfaces with medium (100-grit) sandpaper.

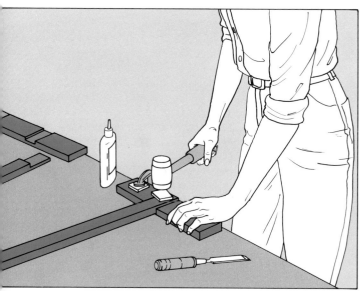

7 **Making the lap joint.** Clamp a base piece to the worktable, and test the lap joint by fitting the notched part of a leg into the notch in the base piece. If the base-piece notch is too narrow, chisel small amounts off each side of the notch. If the outer surfaces of leg and base are not flush when the pieces are lapped, shave small amounts off the face of each notch. When the lap joint is a snug fit, pull it apart and apply carpenter's wood glue to each of the notches. Reassemble the joint and tap the pieces together with the mallet, protecting the wood's surface with a thin wood scrap *(above)*. Clamp the joint to let the glue set. Assemble the second leg and base the same way, then allow the glue to cure overnight.

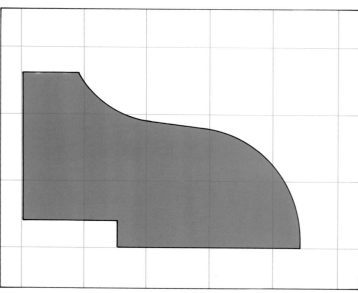

8 **Making the base pattern.** Draw a grid of 1-inch squares on a 5-by-7-inch piece of lightweight cardboard or heavy paper. Using the pattern above as a guide, mark the points where the outline of the base piece crosses the lines of the grid. Connect the marks and copy the pattern, then cut it out with scissors or a utility knife.

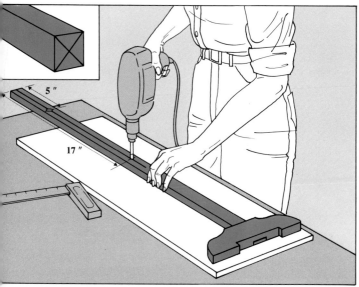

11 **Drilling crossbar holes.** Lay the leg, outside face up, on scrap wood. Mark the midpoint of the leg's width at two places near the top; draw a line through the marks and about halfway down the leg. Mark this center line 5 inches and 17 inches from the top. Wrap a piece of tape ⅜ inch from the tip of a ⅜-inch twist bit, and drill a ⅜-inch-deep hole at each mark. Change to a ³⁄₁₆-inch bit and drill completely through the leg at the center of both holes. Repeat for the second leg. Then, on each end of the two pieces of ¾-inch molding stock, draw an X, running lines from corner to corner to mark the center *(inset)*. Use a ⅛-inch bit, marked with tape 1½ inches from its tip, to make a 1½-inch hole at the center of each X.

12 **Assembling the rack.** Apply a small amount of glue to one end of a molding-stock crossbar. Holding the bar against the top hole at the inside of one leg, drive a 2-inch No. 10 wood screw through the hole and into the end of the bar. Fasten the second crossbar to the leg in a similar fashion. Then glue and screw the second leg to the opposite ends of the attached bars. Cover the heads of the screws by gluing ⅜-inch wood plugs into the holes. Let the glue cure overnight before finishing the wood.

wood plug

A wood tray for the tub

Simplicity itself, the redwood-and-birch soap tray below is essentially a shallow box with sidepieces extended into curved handles that fit over the bathtub rim. The tray makes a stylish and convenient rack for bath-time reading matter or a caddy for sponge and soap. The bottom is a row of dowels that will hold the various bath articles while allowing suds and water to drain away.

The 30-inch-long tray shown here will span most standard tubs; the gently curved handles will fit easily over most tubs' rims. But measure your tub before you begin and, if necessary, alter the length of the sidepieces. For a snugger fit, bend a piece of flexible wire around the rim and transfer the exact curve of your tub to the cardboard pattern you will use to mark the sidepieces *(Step 1)*. If your tub's width varies from one section to another, be sure to measure at the narrowest spot where you plan to use the tray.

The tray is made of four pieces of redwood and six birch dowels, all of which can be cut to size at the lumberyard or at home. However, the redwood pieces are sawed from a 1-by-4 that needs to be ripped — cut along the grain — to create a strip 2¾ inches wide. You can leave the tricky ripping to a professional, then use a miter box and sharp backsaw to cut all the pieces to length. The dowels, inserted through holes drilled in the endpieces, are secured by galvanized 1-inch brad[s].

Use a power drill with a ½-inch bit t[o] make the dowel holes and a saber saw t[o] shape the curved sidepieces. To guara[n]tee a smooth cut, fit the saw with a ¼-inc[h] blade that has 8 to 10 teeth per inch.

The tray should last for years without [a] finish, first turning a streaky black an[d] then, eventually, a uniform driftwoo[d] gray. (Other woods can be substitute[d,] though few share redwood's natural r[e]sistance to rot and decay.) To preserv[e] both the redwood and its original colo[r,] finish the tray with two or three coats [of] polyurethane varnish, or paint it with a[n] oil-based primer and a compatible wate[r-]based top coat.

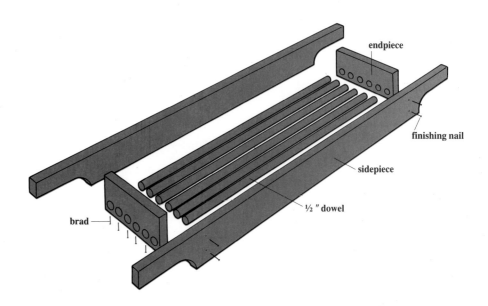

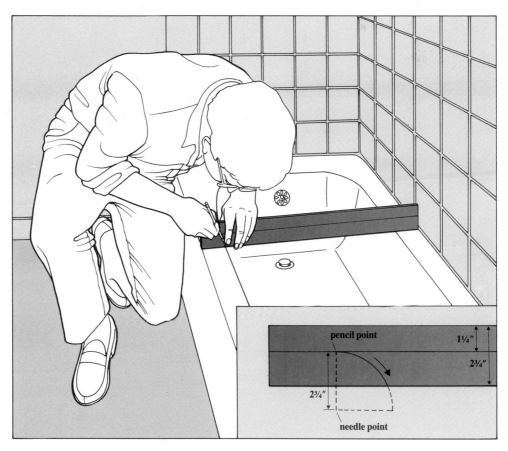

Materials List

Redwood 1 x 4	8 ′ kiln-dried redwood 1 x 4, graded Clear All Heart, ripped to 2¾″ wide, cut into: 2 sidepieces, 30″ long 2 endpieces, 6″ long
Dowels	6 birch dowels, ½″ in diameter, 17½″ long
Nails	8 fourpenny galvanized finishing nails
Brads	12 18-gauge galvanized brads, 1″ long
Filler	redwood-tinted waterproof wood filler

A dowel-bottomed tray. Two 30-inch-long sidepieces butted against two 6-inch-long endpieces frame the tray. The bottom is a row of six ½-inch dowels, cut 17½ inches long and inserted into holes drilled through the endpieces at 1-inch intervals, beginning ½ inch from the sides. The dowel ends are forced flush with the outsides of the end-pieces and secured with galvanized brads before the endpieces and side-pieces are assembled with galvanized finishing nails.

Making a pattern for the sides. Cut a strip of lightweight cardboard 2¾ inches wide and exactly as long as the bathtub is wide — in this case, 30 inches. Draw a line 1¼ inches from what will be the top edge of the strip. Then hold the strip across the tub, and put a tick mark on the bottom where it crosses the inner edge of the rim nearest you; extend this mark up to intersect the line. Next, lay the cardboard on a flat surface. Set a compass to a radius of 2¾ inches. Put the pencil at the intersection and the needle directly below it, as shown in the inset. Draw an arc from the intersection to the edge of the cardboard. Fold the cardboard in half crosswise and cut out the pattern, then test the fit in the tub. ▶

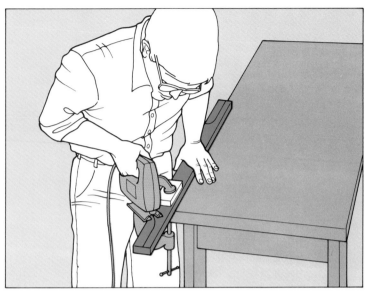

2 **Cutting handles.** Trace the cardboard pattern onto one of the redwood sidepieces. Using a small softwood scrap to protect its surface, clamp the sidepiece to a worktable with the traced pattern up, one end extending over the table's edge. Cut along the outline of the pattern with a saber saw. Turn the piece around and saw along the outline on the other end. Then trace the pattern onto the second sidepiece and cut it. Use coarse (60-grit) sandpaper to sand any cut marks in the sawed edges.

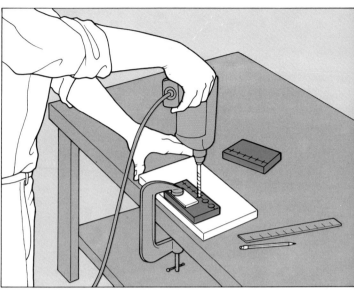

3 **Drilling the dowel holes.** Draw a light pencil line on one face of an end-piece, ½ inch from one long edge. Intersect the line with short tick marks ½ inch from each end and at 1-inch intervals in between. Clamp the endpiece to the worktable, with a long scrap beneath it and a small scrap on top of it. Using a ½-inch bit, drill completely through the wood at the intersecting marks. Repeat this process on the second endpiece.

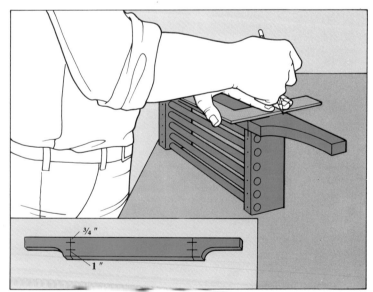

6 **Marking the sides for nailing.** Lay the dowel assembly on its side, dowels toward you, and center a sidepiece on top of it. Directly above the midline of each endpiece, mark the edge of the sidepiece. Then use a carpenter's square to draw a light pencil line from each of the marks across the outside face of the sidepiece. Intersect each of these lines with two tick marks, one ¾ inch down from the top edge, the other 1 inch up from the bottom *(inset)*. Repeat for the other sidepiece.

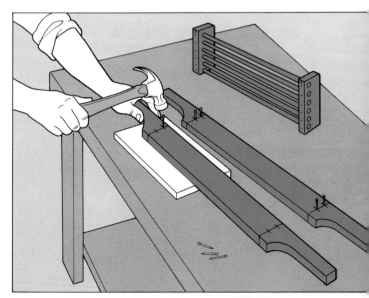

7 **Starting the side nails.** To avoid splitting the wood, blunt the sharp ends of eight fourpenny finishing nails by gently tapping on their points with a hammer. Then drive a blunted nail into, but not through, the wood at each of the four marked spots on each sidepiece.

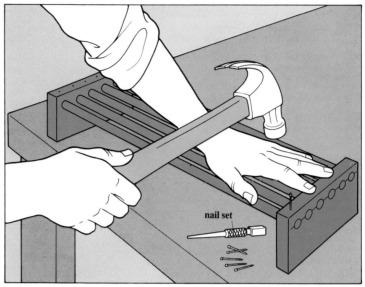

4 **Inserting the dowels.** Lay one endpiece flat on the worktable and insert the dowels into its holes. Then work the other endpiece onto the tops of the dowels, slowly angling the endpiece down and easing the dowels one by one into the holes *(above)*. When all of the dowels are installed, gently tap one endpiece, then the other, with a mallet until the ends of the dowels are flush with the outer faces of the endpieces.

5 **Securing the dowels.** Turn the assembly dowel side upward. Check to see that the dowel ends are flush with the outer faces of the endpieces. Then, splaying your hand to hold the assembly steady, hammer 1-inch brads through the bottoms of the endpieces into the center of each of the dowels. Work from alternate sides toward the middle so that vibrations from the hammering do not skew the assembly. Use a nail set to drive all of the brad heads flush with the wood.

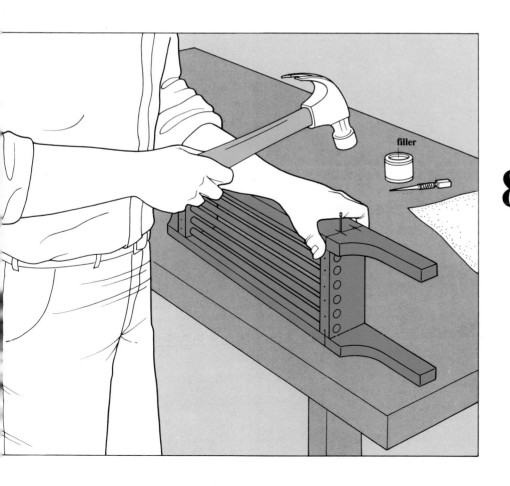

8 **Attaching the sides.** Center a sidepiece over the dowel assembly, making sure that all top and bottom edges are flush. Then, gripping both pieces together, hammer the started nails through the sidepiece and into each endpiece. Turn the tray over and attach the other sidepiece. Use a nail set to recess all nails below the surface of the wood; fill the depressions with redwood-tinted waterproof wood filler. Let the filler dry, and smooth all surfaces with medium (100-grit) and fine (150-grit) sandpaper.

Coordinated fabric accessories

Matching shower curtains to a basin skirt creates an appealing combination. When that decorative pair is fashioned from a fabric that matches the wallpaper — even including the paper's patterned border — the bathroom becomes a veritable paradigm of harmony. Such agreeable fabrics, papers and paper borders are widely available in a wealth of colors, patterns and textures. For simple sewing and maintenance, the best fabric choices are lightweight to medium-weight cottons or cotton blends.

These shower curtains employ an overall cotton print with a printed border fashioned in a classic curtain design: tied-back panels gathered on a rod. A ruffle of fabric heading above the rod casing gives a polished look to the tops of the curtain; a sewed-on border finishes the hems. The tiebacks here are made from the fabric's border design. Rings sewed to their end fit over adhesive-backed plastic hooks mounted on the tiled walls. Whether you make tied-back shower curtains or the more familiar single-panel style (box, page 115), such curtains are strictly decorative. The work of confining water during a shower is done by a plain plastic curtain that hangs on a separate, lower rod and is gathered out of sight behind one of the fabric curtains when not in use.

The skirt for the washbasin is an eminently practical contrivance that covers up plumbing pipes and whatever else is beneath the basin. For the skirt shown here, the fabric is gathered into billowy folds and stitched to a wide band. The top of the skirt is anchored to the basin with adhesive-backed Velcro® tape.

The fabric used here has a border design running alongside the selvages — the tightly woven side edges of the material. Because the borders appear on each curtain's side edges, the side hems consist only of turned-back selvages. If your fabric has no border, put in a double-folded 1½-inch side hem. When widths of fabric are joined to make a curtain panel, the borders are trimmed off the edges that will be seamed together. Here, those cut-off border strips are then stitched to the bottom hems of curtains and skirt.

These curtains hang from a spring-tension rod. In the photograph at left the curtain's top edges are brought even with the top of the window by placing the rod few inches above, and slightly in front of the stationary rod from which the plastic curtain is hung. The spring-tension rod could also be placed directly in front of the stationary rod to hide it.

If instead you make a single large fabric panel to hang in front of a plastic liner on the stationary rod, it will need buttonholes along the top to fit the hooks or rings that support it. Unless you want to sew buttonholes by hand or pay to have them done, you will need a buttonhole attachment for your sewing machine.

Instructions for making tied-back curtains begin at right, those for a straight-hanging curtain on page 115, and the instructions for a basin skirt on page 116.

ied-back Shower Curtains

Measuring. To calculate the fabric needed for a pair of curtains, first install a spring-tension rod — the springs hidden in one end hold it tight. Triple the width of the area to be covered; divide the result by your fabric width and use the nearest even number as the figure for the fabric widths you need. Measure from the top of the rod to the floor and subtract 1½ inches for clearance at the floor. Add 11½ inches for a doubled heading and casing, and 5½ inches for a doubled hem. With patterned fabric, measure lengthwise from one design detail to the next identical detail, and add that amount. Multiply the resulting length by the widths required, then divide by 36 to determine the yards you need.

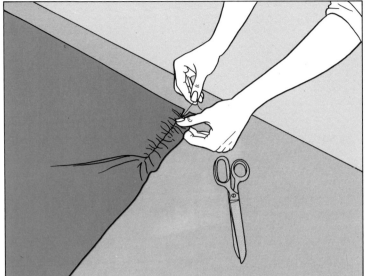

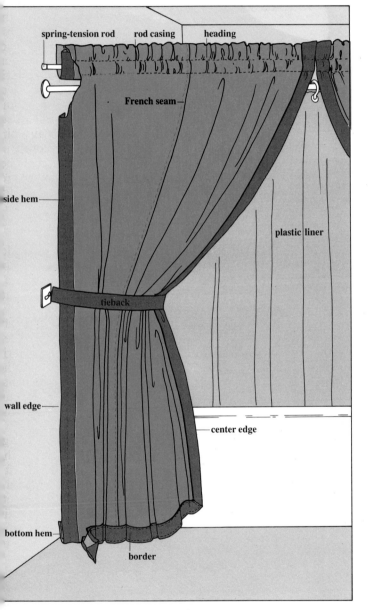

2 **Squaring the fabric.** Lay the fabric flat and clip across a selvage near one end. At the cut, catch a crosswise thread and pull it across the fabric's width, using your other hand to push the fabric away *(above)*. Clip the opposite selvage to remove the thread; cut along the line left behind to form a straight edge. If the thread breaks while you pull it, remove the loose thread, find the broken end and continue pulling it. From the straight edge, measure along the selvage the length needed for each curtain panel. Clip the selvage, pull a thread and cut along the line.

For a printed fabric whose design has not been placed squarely on the fabric, draw a chalk line across the fabric perpendicular to the design; cut along the line. Starting from that line, cut the fabric into lengths.

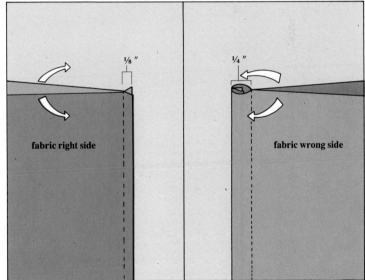

3 **Sewing French seams.** For each fabric length, make a pin line ½ inch inside the inner border edge on all of the fabric edges that will be joined to make the two panels. Trim off the borders along those lines and set aside.

Place two lengths wrong sides together and pin; be sure to match any design details in the fabric. Using a straight seam of 10 to 12 stitches to the inch, first lock-stitch — sew 2 or 3 stitches in place — then stitch ¼ inch from the fabric's raw edges; lock-stitch at the seam's end. Trim the seam allowance to ⅛ inch and press it open. Fold the fabric right sides together *(arrows, above left)* at the seam and press again. Sew another seam ¼ inch from the fold *(above, right)* and press the seam to one side. Use French seams to join the rest of the lengths into two panels. ▶

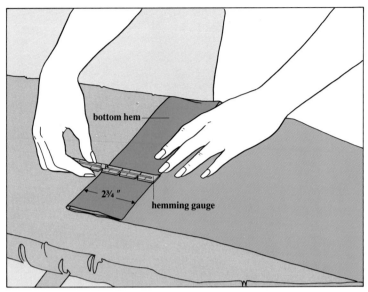

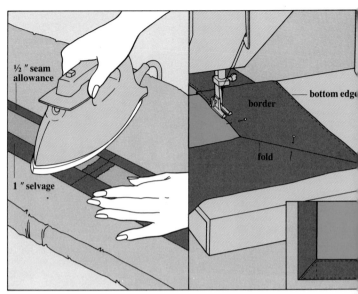

4 **Establishing hems.** Lay each curtain panel in turn wrong side up on an ironing board or padded work surface. Using a hemming gauge, fold over 2¾ inches of fabric at the bottom edge of each panel; press the fold with an iron as you measure across the fabric. Then turn up another 2¾-inch fold to form a double hem *(above)* and press again; now unfold the hem. At the sides of the curtain, fold back the fabric's selvage just to the point where the border design begins; press and pin in place, then refold the bottom hem and pin. At the top edge of each curtain panel, measure and press in a double 4½-inch hem, and pin it in place.

5 **Attaching the bottom border.** Seam together enough sections of the reserved border fabric to make two strips, each 1 inch longer than a curtain panel is wide. Fold back and press the selvage on one long edge of each strip and a ½-inch hem on the other long edge *(above, left)*. Then fold over and press ½ inch of fabric at both ends of each strip. Next, lay one curtain panel at a time right side up. Align the bottom and side edges of one strip with those of the panel; pin. Fold under each end of the strip diagonally *(inset, above right)*, and pin. Stitch across the panel ⅛ inch from its bottom edge, removing the pins as you come to them. Next, stitch the diagonal at one end of the strip, across the top edge *(above, right)*, and down the strip's other diagonal end.

8 **Making tiebacks.** To determine the finished length of each tieback, wrap a cloth tape measure around a curtain panel and hold the tape ends against the wall. Adjust the tape until you achieve the tied-back look you desire; double the measurement on the tape and add 1 inch for seam allowances.

Cut a border strip to this length, fold it in half crosswise — right sides together — and pin around the edges. Beginning at the end fold, stitch along the outside edge of the border pattern, down one side, across the cut end and along the other side to the center. Raise the needle and the presser foot, and pull the tieback under the needle to leave an unsewed opening about 3 inches long. Lower the presser foot and stitch the rest of that side *(right)*. Clip the threads at the opening, turn the tieback right side out and press it. Hand-stitch the opening closed with an overcast stitch. Then center a ⅜-inch bone ring on the edge of each end of the tieback and hand-stitch it in place *(inset)*.

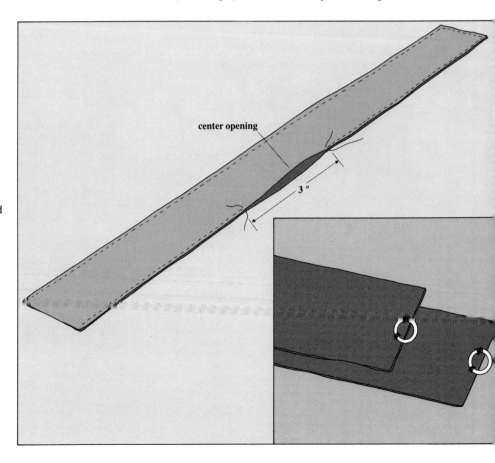

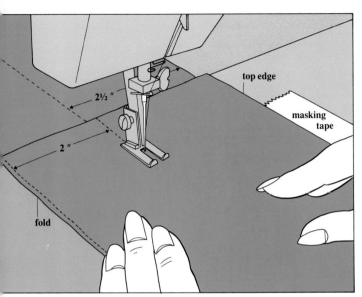

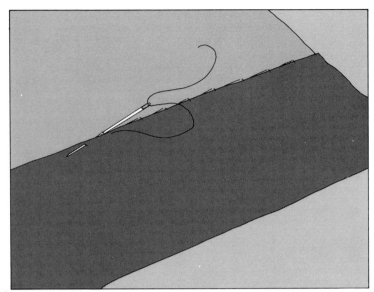

6 **Sewing the heading.** Lay each curtain panel in turn wrong side up. At the top of the curtain panel, stitch a straight seam across the bottom edge of the folded hem, ⅛ inch from the fold; lock-stitch at the beginning and end of the seam. Then, at one side of the curtain, measure down 2½ inches from the hem's top edge and mark that point with a pin. Place the panel under the presser foot at the marking pin; place a strip of masking tape on the machine's throat plate at the edge of the curtain to serve as a guide when stitching the seam. Now stitch once more across the panel *(above)*, lock-stitching at the beginning and end of the seam.

7 **Blind-hem stitching the side hems.** Thread a needle and knot the thread's end. Starting under one end of a side hem to hide the knot, draw the needle up through the edge of the hem. Then pick up one or two threads from the wrong side of the face fabric, close to the hem edge, and slide the needle horizontally for ½ inch; pull the thread through to the top of the hem fabric again *(above)*. Make another stitch in the face fabric and repeat. Sew evenly spaced stitches along the hem edge, then tie off the thread by taking two stitches through the fabric and clipping the thread. Hem the second panel similarly. Then press the finished curtain panels and slide the rod through the casings, gathering up each curtain at an end of the rod. Hang the rod at the tub.

A Conventional Shower Curtain

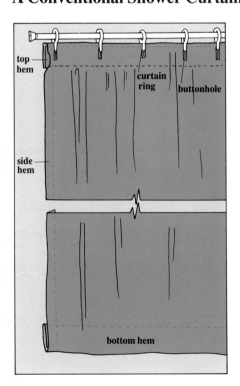

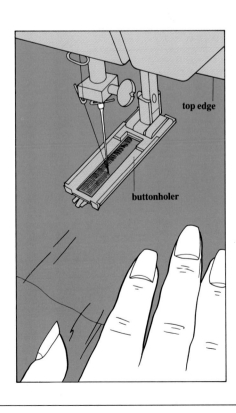

All the sides of a single-panel shower curtain are hemmed and the top is finished with buttonholes for curtain rings. To calculate the fabric needed, first measure the width of the plastic liner that will back it. For a bordered fabric, add 2 inches for side hems; for plain fabric, add 6 inches for double 1½-inch side hems. To determine length, measure from the bottom of the curtain rod to the floor and subtract 1½ inches. Then add 7 inches for a double 1½-inch top hem and a double 2-inch bottom hem. (For a patterned fabric, add one fabric repeat to the length of each fabric width needed to make the curtain.)

Pin the curtain's hems *(Step 4)*; hand-stitch the bottom and side hems *(Step 7)*. Machine-stitch across the top hem of the curtain ⅛ inch from the hem's bottom fold.

Lay the curtain wrong side up and place the top edge of the plastic liner ¼ inch below the curtain's top edge; align the side edges. With a pencil or dressmaker's chalk, mark the positions of the liner's holes on the curtain. Attach the machine's buttonholer and set it for an opening 1 inch long. Practice on a scrap of fabric, then stitch the buttonholes, and slit open the fabric within them. Press the curtain and insert rings through the holes of the curtain and the liner.

A Gathered Skirt for the Washbasin

1 **Anatomy of a basin skirt.** The skirt consists of four elements — a top band, a gathered skirt, a bottom border, and a strip of Velcro® tape securing them all to the basin. To calculate the fabric width needed for the top band, measure around the basin's top edge, from one wall to the other; add 4 inches for side hems. The top band should be 2 to 3 inches deep. If it is made from a fabric border, as here, add ½ inch to allow for one lengthwise seam joining the band and skirt; use the selvage for the hem along the band's top edge. For plain fabric, add 1 inch for seam allowance and hem.

For the gathered-skirt width, triple the wall-to-wall basin measurement. Divide the result by your fabric width and round the figure upward to the next whole number to find how many fabric widths you need. For the skirt length, measure from the basin's top edge to the floor. Subtract 3 inches for the top-band width and the clearance above it; add 6 inches for a hem and seam allowance. Multiply the result by the number of fabric widths and divide by 36 for how many yards of fabric required.

For the skirt's border, border strips may be trimmed from the fabric, or strips 2 to 3 inches wide may be cut from contrasting fabric; the strips then are seamed together in a continuous band that spans the width of the skirt's bottom edge *(Step 2)*.

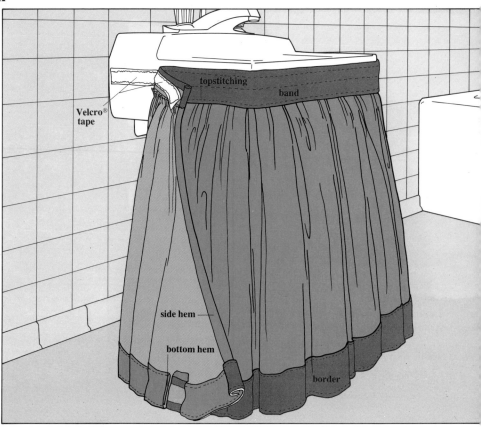

4 **Pinning the skirt and band.** Cut a strip of border fabric to the total length of the skirt's top band *(Step 1)*. Fold over and press the selvage on one long side of the strip and the ½ inch of fabric on the opposite side — leaving only the border design on the fabric's right side. At each end of the strip, fold over and press in a double 1-inch hem; hand-stitch the hems in place. Then measure off the top edge of the skirt and the bottom edge of the band into quarters and mark those points with pins. Lay the two pieces right side down on a flat surface with the pinned edges abutting. Align the pins, bunching the skirt's edge as necessary. Pin the right side of the skirt to the right side of the band's pressed seam allowance at the quarter points *(above)*; do not pin through the cord.

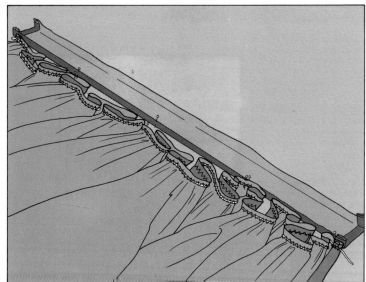

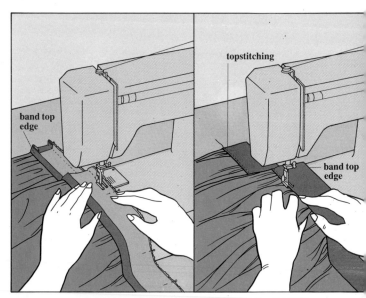

5 **Stitching the band to the skirt.** To gather the top edge of the skirt, pull an end of the nylon cord with one hand; use the other hand to distribute the gathers evenly across the fabric until half of the skirt's top edge fits snugly against the band. Then repeat the action from the skirt's opposite side. Insert additional pins to secure the band to the skirt, then stitch a seam joining the two sections ½ inch from the raw edges *(above, left)*. Press the seam allowance up toward the band. Lay the skirt right side up and topstitch — sew a straight-stitch seam — on the band ¼ inch from the seam line *(above, right)*. This will hold the seam allowances to the back of the band.

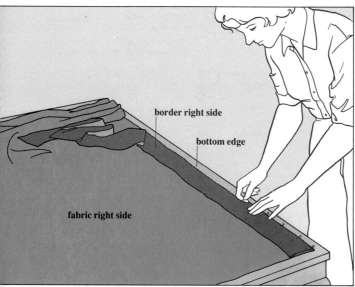

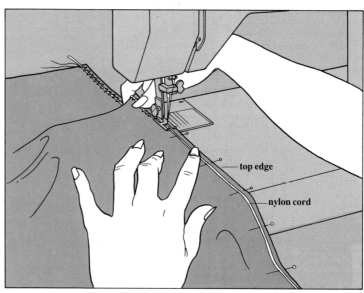

2 **Adding a bottom border.** Square the fabric and cut the fabric lengths needed for the skirt *(page 113, Step 2)*. Trim off the borders plus ½ inch from all the fabric edges and join the lengths *(page 113, Step 3)*. Then measure and press in a double 2¾-inch bottom hem; pin in place. Seam together a border strip equal in length to the width of the skirt. Fold over and press in hems on the long sides of the strip *(page 114, Step 5)*. Next, lay the skirt right side up and place the border on it right side up, aligning the bottom and side edges; pin in place *(above)*. Sew the fabric layers together with seams placed ⅛ inch from the top and bottom edges of the strip. Then, at the side edges of the skirt, fold over and press in a double 1-inch hem; hand-stitch the hem *(page 115, Step 7)*.

3 **Inserting gathering cord.** Cut a piece of nylon cord 2 inches longer than the skirt's width. Starting ¼ inch from the skirt's top edge, pin the cord to the fabric, leaving 1 inch of cord extending past each of the side edges. Set your machine to the widest zigzag stitch setting. Sew across the fabric *(above)*, making sure the thread crisscrosses over the cord and does not stitch through it; remove the pins as you come to them.

6 **Attaching the Velcro tape.** Cut a section of adhesive-backed Velcro tape — loop tape and hook tape supported by a paper backing — to the length of the skirt's top band. Lay the skirt wrong side up. Peel the loop tape from its backing and press it into place ¼ inch from the top edge of the band. Then sew straight-stitch seams along the tape's top and bottom edges.

Next, hold one side of the skirt up to the basin, about ¼ inch below the basin's top edge. Make a pencil mark where the skirt's top edge rests, and measure down ¼ inch; make a second pencil mark. Measure the distance from the bottom of the basin up to the second, lower pencil mark. Draw marks at that height at 6-inch intervals around the basin. (Measuring up from the basin's sharply defined lower edge is more accurate than measuring down from the rounded corner of the top.)

Peel the backing from the hook tape. Beginning at one side of the basin, align the tape's top edge with the marks and press the tape firmly in place around the basin. Then align the tapes on the skirt and the basin, and press the skirt into place *(left)*.

Adding a glass tub enclosure

Keeping a shower's spray under control in a tub can be done elegantly by a glass enclosure like the one shown below. The enclosure's simple silhouette blends with the walls around the tub, and its reflective panels serve as handsome dressing mirrors while concealing the tub interior and its attendant clutter.

In design and installation, tub enclosures are almost identical to shower enclosures. Both are available in myriad styles and materials: The tempered-glass panels may be clear, opaque, tinted or reflective; the aluminum frame may be polished as is, or finished in colors such as gold, bronze and black; and the doors may be hinged, folding or sliding. Both tub and shower enclosures come in kits with complete instructions and all necessary hardware — although you may need to supply appropriate fasteners for your walls (pages 124-125). The installation techniques shown here apply to all enclo-

sures, although some steps may vary.

To be suitable for an enclosure, a bathtub must be situated between two end walls that are not more than 60 inches apart and that are perfectly square with the tub's rim — the most critical element for any enclosure. Before buying an enclosure kit, check the rim and walls with a carpenter's level (ideally a 4-foot level, which will reveal any dips or unevenness in the walls). Then measure between the end walls at the tub's rim and 30 and 57 inches above it.

If the rim and walls differ in level, squareness or straightness by more than ¼ inch — that is, if you must move one end of the level more than ¼ inch to get a perfect reading, or if the distance between the walls varies by more than ½ inch — you will need to buy angled metal filler strips that match your enclosure. Slide the interlocking angled filler strips behind whichever parts of the frame are out of line (Steps 2-4) and adjust the strips until the enclosure is square. If your shower has wall tiles that end below the enclosure's top, you also will need to fit wall fillers behind the frame's side jambs.

After installation, the only maintenance needed by an enclosure is periodic cleaning with a nonabrasive window cleaner. Balky sliding panels generally can be repaired by adjusting and tightening their rollers (Step 5) and cleaning the roller channel in the frame's header bar.

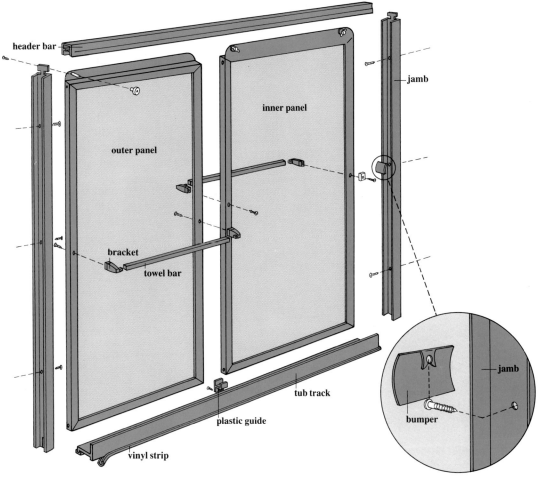

glass tub enclosure. Within a four-piece
[alu]minum frame, two glass panels glide
[sid]eways on rollers that hang from a head-
[er] bar. At the enclosure's sides, jambs
[fas]tened to the walls support the header,
[and] their bumpers *(inset)* cushion the sliding
[pan]els. At the bottom, a track embedded
[in v]inyl strips and caulk seals against water,
[and] a plastic guide keeps the panels
[ali]gned. Each panel is fitted with a towel bar,
[on]e outside the enclosure and one inside.

header bar

jamb

inner panel

outer panel

bracket

towel bar

jamb

tub track

bumper

plastic guide

vinyl strip

slot

groove

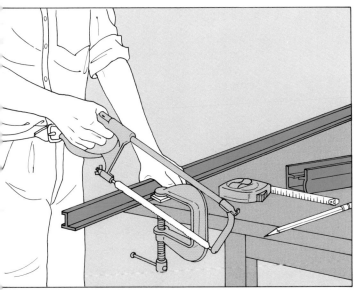

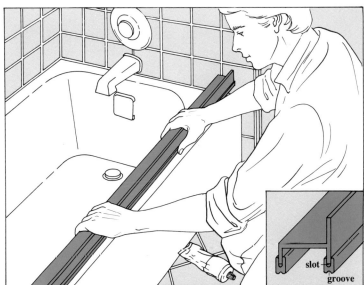

1 **Cutting the pieces.** Measure between the two end walls along the center of the tub's front rim, subtract 1/16 inch and mark the tub track accordingly with a pencil. Clamp the track's wide, flat side to a worktable,
with the track's marked end overhanging the edge; protect the finished
metal from the clamp with a wood scrap. Cut the track at the mark
with a hacksaw *(above)*. Measure between the tub's end walls 57 inches
above the tub's rim, subtract 1/16 inch and cut the header bar to this
length. Smooth the cut ends of the track and header bar with a metal file.

2 **Caulking the tub track.** Use a utility knife to cut two slotted vinyl
strips to the length of the tub track. Press the strips onto the flanges on
the bottom of the track *(inset)*. Center the track on the crosswise dimension of the tub's rim, with the track's tall side toward the room, then
draw a pencil line to mark the track's position. Turn the track over
and apply a continuous bead of acrylic caulk to the exposed grooves in
the vinyl strips. Align the track with the line on the tub's rim and press
lightly until the caulk makes contact with the entire rim *(above)*. ▶

3 **Marking the walls.** Slide the slot at the bottom of one jamb over the track's tall side until the jamb rests on the track *(inset)*. Using a carpenter's level, adjust the jamb until it is plumb; with a pencil, mark the wall through the jamb's screw holes *(above)*. Remove the jamb and drill holes for the appropriate fasteners: 2-inch No. 10 round-head wood screws if you can use a stud; a Molly® bolt for wallboard, acrylic or fiberglass; a ³⁄₁₆-inch plastic wall anchor for tile *(text, page 102)*. Screw the jamb's top and bottom to the wall. Remove the washer from the vinyl door bumper, fasten the washer to the jamb with the middle screw and snap the bumper over the washer *(inset, anatomy drawing, page 119)*. Mark and drill for the other jamb but do not install it yet.

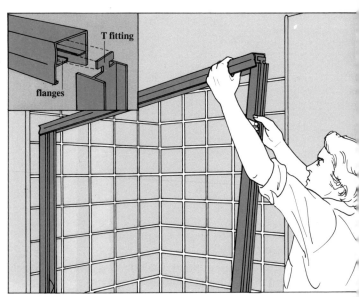

4 **Completing the frame.** Hold the header bar horizontally, its rounded side facing the room; slide the flanges at the header's end under the arm of the T-shaped fitting atop the already-installed jamb. Angle the header's free end slightly outward and slide the top of the uninstalled jamb into the free end *(above)*, with the jamb's bottom slot facing the room. Then slide the jamb down onto the tub track and fasten it to the wall.

5 **Hanging the panels.** Attach two rollers to each panel. Hold each roller over the ledge in the panel's top, insert a roller screw through the center of its diagonal slot and thread it into the roller's shaft. Hold one panel with its rollers facing the tub and lift the panel's top into the header, then lower its rollers onto the header's inner flange. Install the other panel similarly *(above)*, but with its rollers facing the room *(inset)*. Slide each panel sideways until it meets each jamb; if a panel's edges are not parallel to the jambs or if the panel does not glide smoothly, remove the panel from the header and adjust the position of its rollers in their diagonal slots. When the panels are properly aligned, securely tighten each roller screw and rehang the panels.

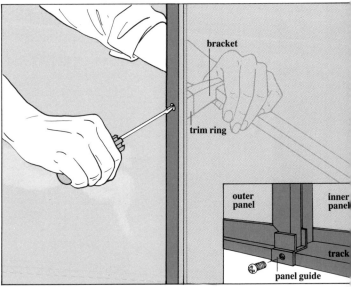

6 **Attaching hardware.** Slip the plastic panel guide onto the center of the track *(inset)*, drill a ⁷⁄₆₄ inch hole through the guide's hole into the track and fasten the guide with a pan-head screw. Fit a trim ring onto the end of each towel-bar bracket and slide the brackets onto the ends of the two towel bars. Fasten a bar to the outer panel by driving screws from inside the tub through the predrilled holes in the panel's frame into the brackets. Slide the inner panel toward the faucet and fasten the other towel bar similarly *(above)*, but secure the bracket next to the faucet with a longer screw that runs through a plastic doorstop as well as the panel's frame. Seal around the jambs and track with acrylic or silicone caulk *(page 84, Step 19)*; let the caulk cure overnight before using the tub.

Using power tools safely

Power tools ranging from saber saws to sewing machines are indispensable aids to a home decorator. If purchased wisely and handled properly, the tools on these pages will ensure excellent results even for the novice.

In general, inferior tools produce inferior work no matter how experienced the operator may be. When you are looking for shop tools, pass by the least expensive ones. At most hardware stores and home-improvement centers, you should be able to find relatively high-quality tools at moderate prices. Look especially for such features as heavy-duty electrical cords, permanently lubricated bearings that simplify tool maintenance, and double-insulated plastic bodies that eliminate the need for a grounded power cord with a three-prong plug. For projects that call for sewing, you need a sewing machine capable of making straight, zig-zag and reverse stitches.

Just as important as buying the right tools is using the proper tool for the job. A saber saw, for example, is designed for cutting curves (below); it can also make long, straight cuts, although a circular saw is usually preferred for those jobs. All power tools come with manufacturer's instructions for care and handling. Take the time to read the instructions, then practice with the tools before you begin a project.

Safety is as important as skill in the operation of power tools, and a few rules apply in every situation:
• Dress for the job. Avoid loose clothing, tuck in your shirt and roll up your sleeves. Tie back your hair if it is long. And wear goggles when there is a possibility that dust or shavings will fly into your eyes — for example, whenever you are sawing or drilling at eye level or overhead. Do not wear gloves when operating power tools; gloves reduce dexterity and can catch in moving parts.

• When operating a power tool, be sure to work on a stable surface; with wood projects, clamp materials to the surface whenever practical.
• Stand comfortably, do not reach any farther than you easily can, and never stand directly in front of — or directly behind — a moving saw blade.

Saws tend to kick back toward the operator if the saw blade gets jammed in the middle of a cut; this generally happens when the sawed section of a workpiece has not been supported as it ought to be to let the saw blade move freely. If the blade should bind while you are making a cut, switch the saw off immediately and support the work to open the cut.

If you are making long cuts in boards or plywood, recruit a helper to support the work for you.
• Always unplug power tools when they are not in use, and whenever you adjust or change parts.

The Saber Saw

Because the blade of a saber saw is only about ¼ inch wide, it can be maneuvered through tight spots and intricate, curved cuts without binding or breaking. With straight cuts, the narrow blade tends to wander from a guideline. But a straightedge guide clamped to the work will help keep such cuts on line.

Your best buy is a variable-speed saw that you can speed up along broad curves and slow down for tricky areas. Blades are sold in sets or individually. Most will cut through wood up to 2 inches thick. Blades with six teeth per inch make fast, rough cuts; blades with 10 to 14 teeth per inch cut more slowly, but also more cleanly. For fine cuts in plywood, buy taper-ground blades with 10 teeth per inch.

To ensure a smooth cut on the good face of a board or panel, work with that surface down. The saber-saw blade cuts on the upstroke, sometimes tearing slivers from the top surface of the work.

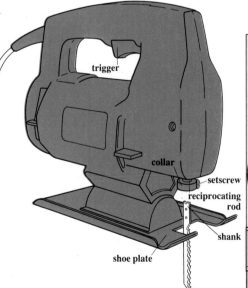

A variable-speed saber saw. A trigger in the handle lets you turn the saw on and off and regulate the speed with which it cuts. To insert a blade, loosen the setscrew in the collar on the reciprocating rod with a screwdriver or a hex wrench, depending on the saw model. Push the notched shank of the blade as far as it will go up into the hollow portion of the reciprocating rod, then retighten the setscrew to anchor the blade.

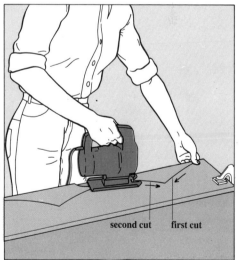

Cutting a curved pattern. Plan cuts so you will not force the blade through an impossibly tight turn; here, both cuts move toward a sharp corner. Rest the tip of the shoe plate on the wood. Start the saw, and guide the blade into the wood, swinging the back of the saw right or left as you move into curves. Do not force the blade, lest it bind or break. If you end a cut with the blade in the wood, let the blade stop before withdrawing it.

The Variable-Speed Drill

Like the saber saw, the variable-speed drill works at a variety of speeds, depending on how hard you squeeze its trigger. Small holes in wood are bored at the fastest speeds; slower speeds are better for drilling large holes in wood and for any hole in metal or masonry.

The ⅜-inch drill at right can accommodate bit shanks from ¹⁄₆₄ inch to ⅜ inch in diameter. Within that range, many different bits are available to drill holes from ¹⁄₆₄ inch to 1½ inches in diameter in wood, metal or masonry. Power drills also can hold the shanks of such accessories as buffing wheels, grinding wheels and hole saws.

The drill is often used to drill the hole for a wood screw that fastens together two boards. This task actually requires three holes: one in the bottom board to grip the screw's threads tightly, and two successively wider holes in the top board for the shank and head. You can use a separate twist bit for each hole, then broaden the top hole with a countersink bit. More simply, you can bore all three holes at once with a counterbore bit, which matches the shape of the screw's threads and shank, and has an adjustable head that bores, or counterbores, a recess for the screw-

head. Avoid cheap counterbore bits: They tend to clog.

Spade bits bore holes up to 1½ inches in diameter; because these bits tend to wobble, use of a drill guide is advisable. The model at right, below, will fit any drill with a threaded shaft.

Masonry bits, with closely spaced, carbide-tipped edges, grind slowly through brick, concrete, and tile, which would quickly dull an ordinary twist bit.

Masonry and spade bits are most often sold singly; countersinks are sold in only one size. Counterbore and twist bits are sold singly and in sets that include the most frequently used sizes.

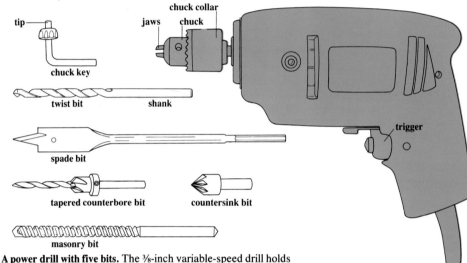

A power drill with five bits. The ⅜-inch variable-speed drill holds twist, spade, counterbore, countersink and masonry bits with shanks up to ⅜ inch in diameter. To insert a bit, turn the chuck collar to open the jaws, push the bit shank between the jaws and tighten the collar by hand until the jaws grip the shank. Then push the tip of the chuck key into one of the three holes in the chuck, and twist the key handle. To change bits, loosen the collar with the chuck key before turning it by hand.

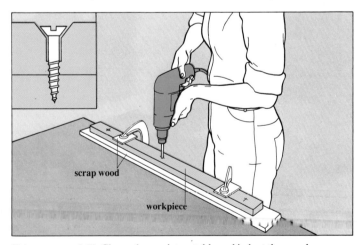

Using a power drill. Clamp the work to a table and indent the wood at the starting point with an awl. To govern a hole's depth, wrap tape around the bit at the required distance from the tip. Set the bit in the dent, squeeze the trigger and push the drill straight down with steady, moderate pressure. To drill holes for a wood screw *(inset),* use a tapered counterbore bit *(above).* Or drill two holes of increasing size, a narrow one in the bottom piece for the screw's threads and a wide one in the top for the shank. Widen the hole's mouth with a countersink bit if it will be puttied, or use a third twist bit if it will be plugged with a short dowel.

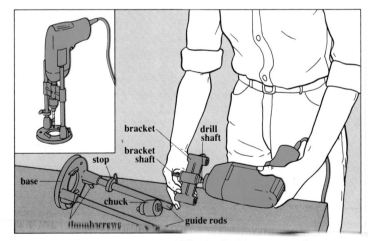

Attaching a drill guide. Remove the drill's chuck. (Most unscrew from the shaft of the drill, but check the manufacturer's instructions.) Twist the guide bracket onto the drill shaft; screw the chuck onto the bracket's shaft. Slip the guide rods through their holes in the bracket, loosen the thumbscrews on the base, set the ends of the rods flush with the bottom of the base, and tighten the screws; this procedure ensures that the holes drilled are perpendicular to the work surface when the drill guide is upright *(inset).* If you want to drill to a certain depth, position the stop on the guide rod after you have inserted a bit in the chuck.

The Sewing Machine

One of the most ingenious home tools, the sewing machine is also one of the easiest to use and maintain. A good machine is virtually trouble-free mechanically and needs only a light oiling every three or four operating hours.

Threading the machine properly is essential; the owner's manual will tell you how. Although every model threads somewhat differently, there are always two threads, an upper thread from the spool and a lower thread wound around the bobbin *(right)*. The tension on the upper thread is adjusted with a knob.

Synthetic thread must be used with synthetic fabric, and natural with natural, so that, in cleaning, the fabric and thread shrink at the same rate. Size 50 thread and a Size 14 needle are best for most fabrics, though heavier thread and a Size 16 needle make stronger seams in thick fabric, such as canvas.

The number of stitches per inch also affects seam strength. The standard number is 12 to 15 stitches per inch, more if very strong seams are needed.

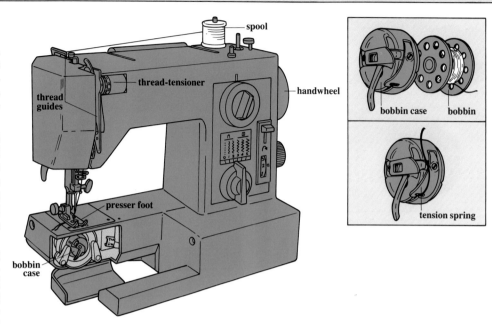

The versatile sewing machine. Every sewing machine has a set of thread guides that take the thread from the spool, through an adjustable thread-tensioner and down to the needle. A second thread is wound around a lower spool called the bobbin *(top inset)* and slipped underneath a tension spring *(bottom inset)* on the bobbin case.

Dials on the machine set the type, length and direction of a stitch. The presser foot, a ski-shaped clamp that holds the fabric flat, comes in a variety of configurations for special stitches. The feed dog, a toothed plate below the presser foot, advances the fabric automatically. The handwheel turns the mechanism to start the first stitch.

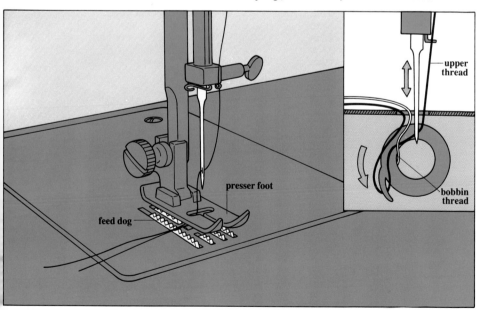

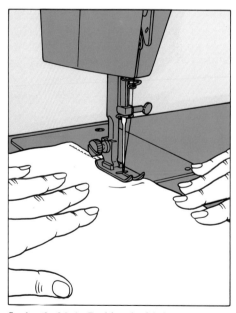

Preparing to sew. After threading the machine, lower the presser foot, grasp the end of the upper thread and turn the handwheel slowly toward yourself. As you do this, the upper thread will tighten around the bobbin thread *(inset)* and pull it up in a loop. Raise the presser foot and pull out the end of the bobbin thread from the loop. Draw out both threads 3 or 4 inches and pull the ends together to the rear of the presser foot.

Sewing the fabric. Position the fabric under the needle. Lower the needle, then the presser foot; turn on the machine and guide the fabric as the feed dog pulls it forward. When you finish sewing, set the machine in reverse and backstitch over the last few stitches. Raise the presser foot, pull out the fabric and cut both threads.

The Basic Fasteners

Locating the skeleton of vertical 2-by-4 studs and horizontal 2-by-10 joists centered every 16 or 24 inches behind your bathroom's walls and ceilings is the first step in hanging or securing many bathroom items. It is also a tricky task that calls for considerable care.

Most commercial stud finders are really magnetic metal detectors that locate studs by the nails in them. These devices are easily deceived by electric cables, wire lath and pipes — all of which a bathroom wall may ha[?] abundance. And most such stud fi[?] do not register at all through tile.

By contrast, an electronic stud f[?] works like sonar, sending out s[?] waves that are reflected back by c[?]

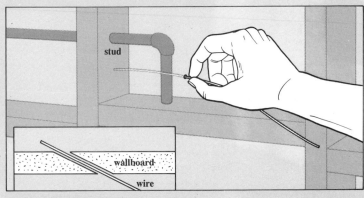

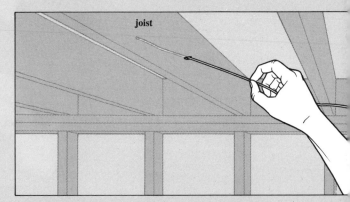

Finding a framing member. With your knuckles, tap lightly across the wall; a solid sound should reveal the approximate position of a wooden stud. To locate a stud precisely, drill a small hole a few inches away from and angled sharply *(inset)* toward the suspected location. Insert a thin, stiff wire until its tip meets the stud. (If you encounter cushiony resistance, the wire is probably running into insulation: Try to push the tip on through.)

Grasp the wire at the hole with thumb and forefinger *(above, left)* to mark the distance from hole to timber. Then extract the wire, and position it at the

same angle outside the wallboard. The wire's tip should now indicate the [?] of the concealed stud; add ¾ inch to find the stud's center. Confirm the lo[?] tion by driving a nail through the wallboard until you feel it enter the woo[?]

Use the same process to locate a joist *(above, right)*. When drilling over[?] head, wear safety goggles to keep plaster dust out of your eyes.

To determine a point anywhere else along the center line of any framing member you have located, measure an equivalent distance from an adjace[?] wall, then confirm by driving a nail.

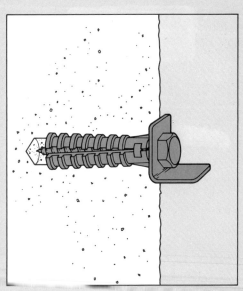

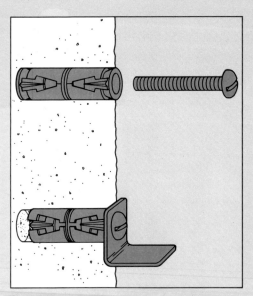

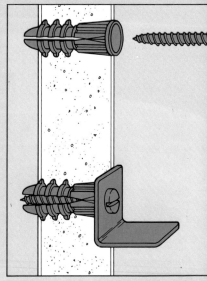

Lag bolt. Sometimes called a lag screw, this big fastener holds a very heavy load. To use it in a stud, drill a pilot hole slightly smaller in diameter than the bolt. Slip the bolt through the hanger of the object to be hung, then drive it into the hole by turning its head with a wrench. In masonry *(shown)*, drill a hole deep enough for the bolt and wide enough so a matching-sized lag shield fits tightly; the flanges at the outer end of the shield should bite into the masonry. Tap the shield into the hole before driving the bolt into the shield.

Expansion shield. This metal device with interior threads is used with a matching machine screw to hold a load on masonry or a thick plaster wall. Drill a hole that will hold the shield snugly, and tap the shield into it. Make sure the screw is long enough to extend through the hanger of the object being hung and the length of the shield. As you tighten the screw, wedges in the shield will be pulled toward the middle, pushing the cylinder sides hard against the masonry or plaster.

Anchor. The sides of an anchor press out to g[?] a tight grip in masonry, wallboard or plaster [?] matching-sized screw is driven into it. A plas[?] anchor *(above)*, sufficient for light loads, can [?] used with a wood screw or a self-tapping scr[?] *(shown)*. Heavier weights need lead anchors. [?] either type, first tap the anchor into a hole drilled to fit it snugly. (In wallboard, as here, [?] anchor and screw should be long enough to e[?] tend through it.) Then insert the screw throu[?] object to be hung, and drive it into the ancho[?]

ojects, even through tile. It locates uds accurately, but it also registers pes, so take plenty of measurements – enough to establish a pattern of uds — and verify them from floor to eiling since some pipes do not extend l the way up the wall.

The most reliable, if painstaking, way o locate framing members is to drill mall holes in the wall or ceiling and robe with a wire *(left)*. If the wall is led, drill just above the tile line or at le ceiling — wherever tiles meet plain alls. For safety, cut off the electricity the bathroom and adjacent rooms at le main switch. Keep the probe holes allow lest you drill through a pipe; if ou do, call a plumber immediately.

If the studs or joists are conveniently cated, nails or wood screws are the asteners of choice. Where framing embers are unavailable, light loads lay be attached with expanding an-ors that grip the edges of holes drilled to the wallboard or plaster. For heav-r loads you need toggle bolts or Molly®

bolts, which cling to a wall or ceiling by squeezing from both sides *(bottom)*.

Other expanding anchors are available for masonry walls, which can bear a load at any point. If the surface of a masonry wall is exposed and you have a choice, the mortar joints are a better place to drill than the brick or block, since mortar is comparatively soft and easy to patch.

In recent years the partition walls of many apartment buildings have been built with metal studs. Self-tapping screws, with sharp threads that hold tightly in sheet metal, are recommended for this type of construction.

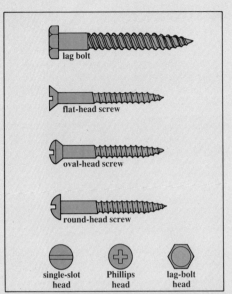

Wood screws. Flat-head screws are countersunk flush with the surface or hidden beneath plugs or putty. Round and oval heads can be left exposed. Heads have one slot or, for a Phillips™ screwdriver, two crossed slots. Phillips heads are less likely to rip under turning pressure. Screw-shaft diameters are denoted by gauge numbers: The higher the number, the larger the diameter. Diameters of lag bolts, whose hexagonal *(shown)* or square heads are turned by wrenches, are expressed in inches (from ¼ to 1 inch).

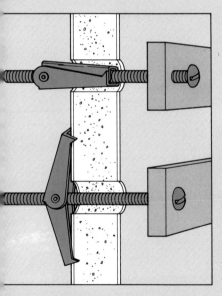

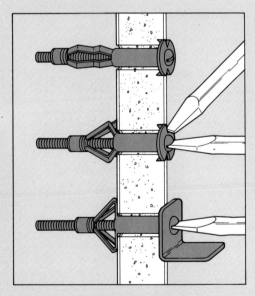

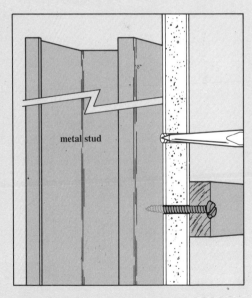

le bolt. A toggle bolt must be long enough s wings to spring open and grip the inside of a w wall. Drill a hole large enough for the d wings to pass through, but do not push them his stage. Unscrew the wings from the slip the bolt through the object to be hung, eplace the wings. Then push the bolt gh the wall; when the wings pop open, the vill feel loose in the hole. Pull the device so that the wings will bite into the inside of the as you tighten the bolt.

Molly bolt. The unbroken cylinder near the bolthead of one of these hollow-wall anchors should be as long as the wall is thick. Tap the Molly bolt into a hole drilled to its diameter. Wedge a screwdriver into one of the indentations in the flange to keep the sheath from turning as you tighten the bolt with another screwdriver. The sheath arms will splay out against the inside of the wall. Do not overtighten, or you may break the Molly bolt's arms. Remove the bolt to put the load on it, then screw it back into position.

Self-tapping screw. This sort of screw is used to attach weights to metal studs. Drill a small hole in the wallboard to the face of the stud. Make a starter dent in the stud with a center punch and a hammer. Then use a twist bit to drill a pilot hole half the diameter of the screw through the thin metal. Insert the screw through the object you are hanging, and drive it into the stud; the screw should be long enough to reach about ½ inch beyond the face of the stud.

Acknowledgments

The index was prepared by Louise Hedberg. The editors are particularly indebted to Lynn Addison, Hyattsville, Maryland; David A. Bennett, Alexandria, Virginia; Rebecca Brandt, Washington, D.C.; Emily Erickson, Out of Hand, Alexandria, Virginia; Betty Anne Ferguson, Springfield, Virginia; Dixie Kaufman, Rocky Road to Kansas, Alexandria, Virginia; Maurice Palmer, M. R. Palmer Construction, Inc., Alexandria, Virginia; Patricia Silaghi, Alexandria, Virginia. For their help in the preparation of this volume, the editors also thank: Acker Brothers, Inc., Kensington, Maryland; David Adamusko, Antique Furniture Restorations, Arlington, Virginia; Marirosa Ballo, Milan; Suzan J. Bartholomew, Summitville Tiles, Inc., Washington, D.C.; Richard Bauer, Toledo Plate and Window Glass Co., Toledo, Ohio; Carla De Benedetti, Milan; Craig Boulter, Century Tile, Inc., Alexandria, Virginia; Emmett Bright, Rome; Sally Coler, The Tile Gallery Inc., Washington, D.C.; Rex Downey, Oxon Hill, Maryland; Franklin Marble & Tile Co., Capitol Heights, Maryland; Isidoro Genovese, Rome; Lucy Globus, Hill and Knowlton, Inc., New York; Charles Goldberg, Union Hardware's Decorator Center, Washington, D.C.; Sari Greenfield, The Tile Gallery Inc., Washington, D.C.; Linda Handmaker, Arlington, Virginia; Russell J. Helwick, Irvine, California; L. E. Hopkins, Corian Building Products Group, E. I. du Pont de Nemours & Company, Inc, Wilmington, Delaware; Jack P. Hough, Rohm Haas, Bristol, Pennsylvania; Horst Huttner, Bla Inc., Alexandria, Virginia; William G. Miller J Alexandria, Virginia; David Mlinaric, Londo Noel Jeffrey Inc., New York; Florence Perch New York; Scott Roos, ALKCO, Franklin Park, Il nois; Earl R. Print, General Electric Compan Cleveland, Ohio; Mark Seaton, Color Tile, Alexa dria, Virginia; Summitville Tiles, Inc., Alexandri Virginia; W. T. Weaver and Sons, Inc., Washin ton, D.C.; Ernest Wesley, Washington, D.C.; Ro ney Wessell, San Francisco, California; Kathy Wi mar, Placewares, Alexandria, Virginia.

Picture Credits

The sources for the photographs in this book are listed below, followed by the sources for the illustrations. Credits from left to right on a single page or a two-page spread are separated by semicolons; credits from top to bottom are separated by dashes.

Photographs: **Cover:** Larry Sherer, photographer / location, courtesy Ernst Alexander. **2, 3:** Aldo Ballo, photographer / Gabriella Giuntoli, architect, Milan. **4:** Giovanna Piemonti, photographer / Ascarelli, Maciocchi, Nicoloa and Parisio, architect, Rome. **5:** © Norman McGrath, photographer / design by Noel Jeffrey, New York. **6, 7:** Derry Moore, photographer / design by David Mlinaric, London. **8:** Larry Sherer, photographer / design by Ernst Alexander, Washington, D.C. **9:** © Norman McGrath, photographer / design by Noel Jeffrey, New York. **10:** Henry Groskinsky, photographer / design by Noel Jeffrey, New York. **11:** Aldo Ballo, photographer / Piero Pinto, architect, Milan. **25:** Larry Sherer, photographer / fixture and fittings: W. T. Weaver and Sons, Inc., Washington, D.C. **26:** Larry Sherer, photographer / fixture and fittings: W. T. Weaver and Sons, Inc., Washington, D.C. — Larry Sherer, photographer / fixture and fittings: Masterworks, Inc., Fairfax, Virginia. **38:** Larry Sherer, photographer / fixture and fittings: W. T. Weaver and Sons, Inc., Washington, D.C. **42:** Larry Sherer, photographer / Maurice Palmer, contractor, Alexandria, Virginia. **50:** Larry Sherer, photographer / courtesy The Tile Gallery Inc., Washington, D.C. **52:** Dan Cunningham, photographer / location, courtesy John and Margaret Yaglenski. **55:** Larry Sherer, photographer / location, courtesy Ernst Alexander. **60:** Larry Sherer, photographer / lights: Lincandescents™ by ALKCO, Franklin Park, Illinois / lavatory: W. T. Weaver and Sons, Inc., Washington, D.C. / towel: J. C. Penney / accessories: Placewares. **64:** Larry Sherer, photographer / towels: J. C. Penney / vanity and fittings: Acker Brothers, Kensington, Maryland. **68, 69:** Walter Smalling Jr., photographer / design by Patricia Silaghi, Alexandria, Virginia. **76:** Larry Sherer, photographer. **78:** Larry Sherer, photographer / courtesy The Tile Gallery Inc., Washington, D.C. / towels: J. C. Penney. **86:** Larry Sherer, photographer / tile: Summitville Tiles, Inc. **89:** Michael Latil, photographer / towels: J. C. Penney / plastic shelves: Blair, Inc. **92:** Dan Cunningham, photographer / jars: Portside, Alexandria, Virginia / towels: J. C. Penney. **96:** Tom Tracey, photographer / design by Rodney Wessell, San Francisco, California. **102:** Larry Sherer, photographer. **103:** Larry Sherer, photographer / hardware: Placewares. **104:** Dan Cunningham, photographer. **108:** Larry Sherer, photographer / location, courtesy Ernst Alexander / accessories: Caswell-Massey, Inc., Alexandria, Virginia. **112:** Dan Cunningham, photographer / design by Augusta Moravek, Bethesda, Maryland / location, courtesy Mr. and Mrs. Thomas Higginson. **118:** Dan Cunningham, photographer / towels: J. C. Penney.

Illustrations: **16-23:** Drawings by Fred Holz, inked by Frederic F. Bigio from B-C Graphics. **25-33:** Drawings by William J. Hennessy Jr., inked by Frederic F. Bigio from B-C Graphics. **34-37:** Drawings by Jack Arthur, inked by Walter Hilmers Jr. from HJ Commercial Art. **39-41:** Drawings by William J. Hennessy Jr., inked by Frederic F. Big from B-C Graphics. **43-49:** Drawings by Jack A thur, inked by Frederic F. Bigio from B-C Graphic **50, 51:** Drawings by Jack Arthur, inked by Arezo K. Hennessy. **53, 54:** Drawings by Greg DeSant inked by Adisai Hemintranont from Sai Graphis. 5 **59:** Drawings by George Bell, inked by Arezou Hennessy. **61-63:** Drawings by Fred Holz, inked Frederic F. Bigio from B-C Graphics. **65-67:** Dra ings by Roger Essley, inked by John Massey. **69-7** Drawings by Roger Essley, inked by Walter H mers Jr. from HJ Commercial Art. **77:** Drawings Greg DeSantis, inked by Elsie J. Hennig. **79-8** Drawings by Fred Holz, inked by Arezou K. He nessy. **86, 87:** Drawings by Fred Holz, inked Walter Hilmers Jr. from HJ Commercial Art. **88-9** Drawings by William J. Hennessy, inked by Elsie Hennig. **93-95:** Drawings by George Bell, inked Adisai Hemintranont from Sai Graphis. **97-10** Drawings by George Bell, inked by Frederic Bigio from B-C Graphics. **102, 103:** Drawings Greg DeSantis, inked by Adisai Hemintranont fro Sai Graphis. **104-107:** Drawings by Roger Essle inked by Elsie J. Hennig. **109-111:** Drawings by Jo S. McGurren, inked by Frederic F. Bigio from B-Graphics. **113-117:** Drawings by Joan McGurre inked by Adisai Hemintranont from Sai Graphi **119, 120:** Drawings by Greg DeSantis, inked Elsie J. Hennig. **121, 122:** Drawings by Roger Es ley, inked by Frederic F. Bigio from B-C Graphic **123:** Drawings by Jack Arthur, inked by Walt Hilmers Jr. from HJ Commercial Art. **124, 12** Drawings by Roger Essley, inked by Frederic Bigio from B-C Graphics.

Index

Time-Life Books Inc. offers a wide range of fine recordings, including a *Big Bands* series. For subscription information, call 1-800-621-7026, or write TIME-LIFE MUSIC, Time & Life Building, Chicago, Illinois 60611.